The Nation's #1 Educational Publisher

McGraw·Hill
Learning Materials
SPECTRUM
SPELLING

Grade 5

Author

Nancy Roser
Professor, Language and Literacy Studies
Department of Curriculum and Instruction
The University of Texas at Austin

McGraw·Hill
Learning Materials

250 Old Wilson Bridge Road
Worthington, Ohio 43085

The McGraw·Hill Companies

EAN

D1424993

Credits

Illustrations: Steve McInturff
Electronic Illustrations: Jennie Copeland, Tom Goodwin
Heads: John Kurtz
Handwriting: Theresa Caverly

McGraw-Hill
Consumer Products

A Division of The *McGraw-Hill* Companies

Send all inquiries to:
McGraw-Hill Learning Materials
250 Old Wilson Bridge Road
Worthington, Ohio 43085

ISBN 1-57768-165-7

How to Study a Word

1 Look at the word.

What does it mean?
How is it spelled?
Is it spelled as you expect?
Are there any unusual spellings?

disappear

2 Say the word.

What vowel and consonant sounds
    do you hear?
Are there any silent letters?

disappear

3 Think about the word.

How is each sound spelled?
Do you see any familiar word parts?

dis/ap/pear

4 Write the word.

Did you copy all the letters carefully?
Did you think about the sounds
    and letters?

disappear

5 Check the spelling.

Did you spell the word correctly?
Do you need to write it again?

disappear

Contents

Lesson   **Page**

1 Spelling the Short *a* Sound 2

2 Spelling the Short *e* Sound 6

3 Spelling the /o/ and /ô/ Sounds 10

4 Spelling the Short *i* Sound 14

5 Spelling the Short *u* Sound 18

6 Review 22

7 Spelling the Long *a* and Long *e* Sounds 24

8 Spelling the Long *o* and Long *i* Sounds 28

9 Spelling the /ü/ and /ū/ Sounds 32

10 Spelling the /ûr/ Sound 36

11 Easily Misspelled Words 40

12 Review 44

13 Spelling Consonant Blends 46

14 Spelling the /ou/ Sound 50

15 Spelling the Final /əl/ Sound 54

16 Spelling the /ôr/ and /är/ Sounds 58

17 Spelling Homophones 62

18 Review 66

iv

19 Spelling Words with *-ed* or *-ing* 68

20 Spelling More Plurals 72

21 Spelling Words Beginning *a* or *be* 76

22 Spelling Singular and Plural Possessive Nouns ... 80

23 Spelling the Names of Body Parts 84

24 Review 88

25 Spelling Words with the Prefix *dis-* or *mis-* 90

26 Spelling Unstressed Vowels 94

27 Spelling Words with *-ent* and *-ant* 98

28 Spelling Compound Words 102

29 Spelling Discoveries and Inventions 106

30 Review 110

31 Spelling Words with Silent Letters 112

32 Spelling Words with *ph* or *gh* 116

33 Spelling the *-tion, -sion,* or *-sure* Endings 120

34 Spelling the Names of Units of Measure 124

35 Spelling the Names of National Parks 128

36 Review 132

Steps in the Writing Process 134

How To Use the Dictionary 136

Speller Dictionary 138

1 Spelling the Short a Sound

CORE

1. jazz
2. cancel
3. lantern
4. blanket
5. tractor
6. travel
7. shampoo
8. paddle
9. castle
10. magnet
11. salad
12. palace
13. catalog
14. cabin
15. cabinet

CHALLENGE

16. handsome
17. plaid
18. handicap
19. anchor
20. casserole

Sound	Sign	Spelling
short a	/a/	magnet

Say each word. Listen for the short a sound.

Study the spelling. How is the short a sound spelled in *jazz*?

Write the words.

1–15. Write the Core Words. Circle the letter that spells the short a sound.

16–19. Write the Challenge Words that have the short a sound spelled a. Circle the letter that spells the short a sound.

20. Write the Challenge Word that has the short a sound spelled in another way. Circle the letters that spell the short a sound.

SPELLING TIP
The short a sound is often spelled a.

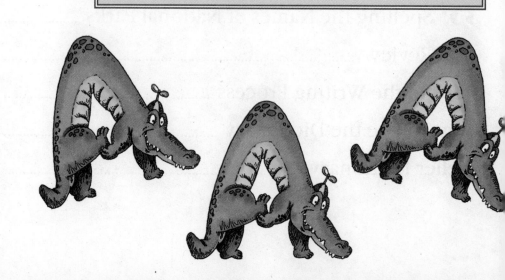

Words and Meanings

Write the Core Words that best complete the story.

All That Jazz

Music has always attracted people like a (1). In the Middle Ages, a harp would delight the king and queen in their (2). In American pioneer days, a family in a one-room (3) would sing and dance to fiddle music by the light of a (4).

Today people listen to music while they (5) their hair, eat a (6), or browse through the pages of a (7). They listen as they (8) by car or (9) a canoe. They listen in a concert hall or while sitting on a (10) on the grass.

Music is often part of the workday, too. A farmer may listen to the radio while driving a (11). A carpenter may listen while building a kitchen (12).

People enjoy all kinds of music, from modern (13) to the ancient court music once performed at the royal (14). Rock music is most popular with young people, who will (15) any other plans in order to see their favorite group.

Adding -ed and -ing

Adding -ed or -ing to a word that ends with el or er can be tricky. Double the final l or r only if the last syllable of the base word is stressed.

modeled	referring

Join the words and the word endings.

16. cancel + ed =   18. prefer + ing =   20. offer + ing =
17. travel + ing =   19. propel + ed =

Face the Music

The code below shows the notes of a musical scale. Use the code to read the music. Use both the letters below the scale and the letters of the notes. On a separate piece of paper, write each Core Word you find.

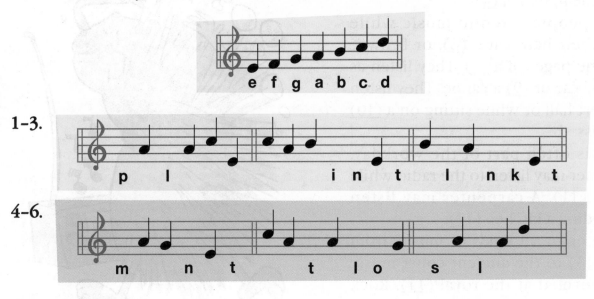

e f g a b c d

1-3.   p   l   i   n   t   l   n   k   t

4-6.   m   n   t   t   l   o   s   l

Take a Close Look   Write Core Words to answer the questions.

7. Which word ends with a double consonant?
8. Which word ends with the /ər/ sound?
9. Which word is the base word for another word?
10. Which word ends with a consonant blend?
11. Which word ends with a double vowel?
12-13. Which words have the final /əl/ sound spelled *le?*
14-15. Which words have the final /əl/ sound spelled *el?*

Use the Dictionary   Study the pronunciation key on any page of your Speller Dictionary. Then write the Core Word for each pronunciation below.

16. kab ′ in   17. kab ′ ə nit   18. kan ′ səl   19. kas ′ əl   20. kat ′ ə log ′

Write some new words for the song "On Top of Old Smokey." Use at least four Core Words from this lesson.

Proofreding prakticee

a (correction over "o")
c (correction over "k")

1-4. Here is a draft of the song words that one student wrote. Find four misspelled Core Words and write them correctly.

On top of a blankit
While camping with Dad,
We ate tuna sallad,
But the tuna was bad.
So we had to cansel
Our trip to the shore.
No way could we travil
With stomachs so sore.

Now proofread your own song words and correct any errors.

CORE			CHALLENGE
jazz	travel	salad	handsome
cancel	shampoo	palace	plaid
lantern	paddle	catalog	handicap
blanket	castle	cabin	anchor
tractor	magnet	cabinet	casserole

2 Spelling the Short e Sound

FOCUS

Sound	Sign	Spelling	
short e	/e/	bench	health

Say each word. Listen for the short e sound.

Study the spelling. How is the short e sound spelled in *bench*? How is it spelled in *health*?

Write the words.

1–9. Write the Core Words that have the short e sound spelled e.

10–15. Write the Core Words that have the short e sound spelled ea.

16–20. Write the Challenge Words. Circle the letters that spell the short e sound.

SPELLING TIP
The short e sound is often spelled e or ea.

CORE

1. bench
2. health
3. swept
4. feather
5. kennel
6. meant
7. plenty
8. welcome
9. sweater
10. tennis
11. sense
12. breath
13. guest
14. leather
15. enemy

CHALLENGE

16. necessary
17. centipede
18. president
19. pennant
20. vegetables

Words and Meanings

Write the Core Words that best complete the story.

Health Quest

The (1) for health brings worthwhile results. When you are in good (2), you wake up and (3) each new day. You say, with (4) of energy, "This is the way life is (5) to be!"

Staying healthy is mostly a matter of common (6). Eat wholesome foods without too much fat. Extra weight can be an (7) of good health. But don't get so thin that you could be (8) away like a pigeon (9) in the wind!

Dress sensibly, too. If you are chilly, put on a (10) or a (11) jacket.

If you often get short of (12), you may need more exercise. Even dogs in a (13) are given a chance to exercise every day. Take up a sport such as (14), and don't spend all your time sitting on a (15).

Irregular Past Tense

You often form the past tense of a verb by adding *-ed*—but not always. Match up these present and past tense verbs by writing them in pairs.

give/gave

16–18. meant   taught   swept
        sweep   mean   teach

Fix the Signs

The Core Words in these store signs have lost some letters. Figure out what letters are missing from each sign and write the complete Core Word. Begin each word with a capital letter.

1.

Lucky Dog
K n l

2.
R.U.
Eatingwell
eal
Foods

3.

Good Yarn
SW TE SHOP

4.
PARK
B N H
Café

5.
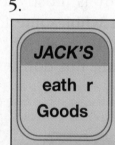
JACK'S
eath r
Goods

6.

Costalot
T n is
and
Swim Club

Add, Subtract, and Spell

Add and subtract letters to spell Core Words. Write each Core Word.

7. s l e e t
    −l −e
    +w +p
    _____

8.   e a s t
    +q +u −a
    _____

9. p r e t t y
    −r −t
    +l +n
    _____

10. s e n d
    −s   −d
       +e +m +y
    _____

11. r e a d
    +b   −d +t +h
    _____

12. f r i g h t
    −r −i −g   −t
    +e +a +t   +e +r
    _____

Complete the Rhymes

Write the Core Word that completes each rhyme.

13. Jane knows jokes and likes to tell some,
    Even when her jokes aren't ___.

14. My gift will please the one it's sent to—
    If I sent the one I ___ to!

15. Don't be nervous, don't be tense.
    Just try hard and use good ___.

Write a paragraph about an activity that helps you stay healthy. Explain why this activity is good for you. Follow the writing process steps on pages 134–135 to write your paragraph. Use at least four Core Words from this lesson.

Prooofreding prakticee

1–4. Here is a draft of one student's paragraph. Find four misspelled Core Words and write them correctly.

> After school I often play basketball with my friends. this is good for my helth because it gives me pleanty of exercise. Exercise is important because without it, my muscles get weak. But when I am out of breth, I have enough sence to sit on a bench and rest for a while.

5–6. This student forgot to capitalize one letter and left out a punctuation mark. Copy the paragraph and correct the errors.

Now proofread your own paragraph and correct any errors.

CORE			CHALLENGE
bench	meant	sense	necessary
health	plenty	breath	centipede
swept	welcome	quest	president
feather	sweater	leather	pennant
kennel	tennis	enemy	vegetables

3 Spelling the /o/ and /ô/ Sounds

CORE

1. collar
2. cause
3. comet
4. awful
5. congress
6. thought
7. proper
8. broad
9. caught
10. common
11. fought
12. prompt
13. bought
14. promise
15. ought

CHALLENGE

16. modern
17. colony
18. crocodile
19. trombone
20. honest

Sound	Sign	Spelling		
short *o*	/o/	comet		
	/ô/	cause	**aw**ful	tho**ugh**t
		br**oa**d	c**augh**t	

Say each word. Listen for the short *o* sound. Listen for the /ô/ sound.

Study the spelling. How is the short *o* sound spelled in *comet*? How is the /ô/ sound spelled in *cause, awful, thought, broad,* and *caught*?

Write the words.

1–7. Write the Core Words that have the short *o* sound.

8–15. Write the Core Words that have the /ô/ sound. Circle the letters that spell the /ô/ sound.

16–20. Write the Challenge Words. Circle the letter that spells the short *o* sound.

SPELLING TIP

The short *o* sound is often spelled *o*. The /ô/ sound can be spelled *au, aw, ough, oa,* or *augh.*

WORDS and MEANINGS

Write the Core Words that best complete the story.

Common Copy

The newspaper is a wonderful source of information. Because it costs so little, it can be (1) by nearly everyone. Many people have it delivered every day. We even learn to expect (2) delivery by the carrier.

Newspapers cover a very (3) range of topics. One article might discuss a law passed by our (4). It will tell us which senators (5) the law was a good idea and which ones (6) against it. Another article might describe how an (7) criminal was finally (8). Still another story might explain the (9) of a war in Asia. A letter to the editor might complain that the mayor broke a (10) to the voters. A personal advice column might suggest the (11) way to handle a problem that many people share in (12). The fashion page might say what kind of shirt (13) is in style or how long skirts (14) to be. A science article might even tell us where to look in the sky for a (15).

Negative Prefixes

The prefixes *im-*, *un-*, *dis-*, *mis-*, and *in-* are negative prefixes. When you add them to a word, you create a new word that means the opposite of the base word. Write a short definition for each word below.

16. improper
17. uncommon
18. disobey

19. mistrust
20. incomplete

Word Play

Correct the Headlines Each newspaper headline below is missing a word. Write the Core Word that makes the most sense in each headline.

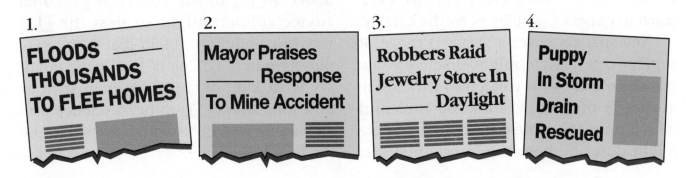

1.
FLOODS ——— THOUSANDS TO FLEE HOMES

2.
Mayor Praises ——— Response To Mine Accident

3.
Robbers Raid Jewelry Store In ——— Daylight

4.
Puppy ——— In Storm Drain Rescued

Build with Syllables Put these syllables together to form seven Core Words. You will need to use one syllable twice. Write the Core Words.

5–11.

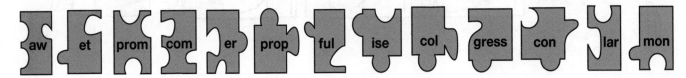

aw   et   prom   com   er   prop   ful   ise   col   gress   con   lar   mon

Get to the Core Write Core Words to answer each question.

12–14. Which three Core Words contain the same shorter Core Word?
15. What is that shorter Core Word?

Use the Dictionary To find a full dictionary definition for a past tense verb, you usually have to look up the base form of the verb. Write the word you would look up to find the definition of these past-tense verbs.

16. thought   17. brought   18. caught   19. fought   20. bought

WRITE ON YOUR OWN

Write a short news story about something interesting that happened recently. It could be a world, town, or personal event. When you write, follow the writing process steps on pages 134–135. Use at least four Core Words from this lesson.

Prooofreding prakticee

1-5. Here is a draft of a news story that one student wrote. Find five misspelled Core Words and write them correctly.

> On Tuesday night, an apartment at 974 Main cought fire. The Fire Department was very promt about putting out the fire. However, the damage to the building was awfull. One firefighter thought that an old space heater may have been the cawse. "People aught to check those things," he said.

Now proofread your own news story and correct any errors.

CORE			CHALLENGE
collar	thought	fought	modern
cause	proper	prompt	colony
comet	broad	bought	crocodile
awful	caught	promise	trombone
congress	common	ought	honest

4 Spelling the Short *i* Sound

CORE

1. quilt
2. mystery
3. glimpse
4. igloo
5. myth
6. limit
7. built
8. blizzard
9. whistle
10. imitate
11. system
12. width
13. simple
14. visit
15. thrift

CHALLENGE

16. instinct
17. typical
18. biscuit
19. gymnast
20. mischief

Sound	Sign	Spelling		
short *i*	/i/	thrift	bu**i**lt	m**y**th

Say each word. Listen for the short *i* sound.

Study the spelling. How is the short *i* sound spelled in *thrift*, *built*, and *myth*?

Write the words.

1–10. Write the Core Words that have the short *i* sound spelled *i*.

11–12. Write the Core Words that have the short *i* sound spelled *ui*.

13–15. Write the Core Words that have the short *i* sound spelled *y*.

16–20. Write the Challenge Words. Circle the three words that have the short *i* sound spelled two different ways.

SPELLING TIP
The short *i* sound can be spelled *i*, *ui*, or *y*.

WORDS and MEANINGS

Write the Core Words that best complete the story.

An Igloo Is Built

The idea of a house made of snow seems magical, like something out of a fairy tale or (1). But if you ever (2) the arctic region, you may get a (3) of a real snowhouse. It is called an (4).

Igloos are (5) from blocks of snow. Why people built with snow is not a (6). In fact, the reason is (7). There is a (8) to the resources available in arctic areas. Snow is the only resource that does not have to be used with great (9).

To build an igloo, you can (10) the same method or (11) some animals use when they burrow holes in the snow for warmth. You just have to know just what height and (12) to make the blocks of snow.

An igloo is the best kind of shelter to be in during an arctic (13). When the winds (14) across the snowy plains, an igloo can keep you as cozy as a soft, warm (15).

Adjective Suffixes -ous and -y

Change each noun to an adjective by adding the suffix -ous or -y. If the noun ends in y, change the final y to i before adding the suffix.

16. mystery
17. thrift
18. might

19. glory
20. fruit

Word Play

Decode the Blocks Each snow block holds a word and a number. If the number in a block is 1, write down the first letter of the word in the block. If the number is 2, write down the second letter, and so on. Then unscramble the letters from the row of blocks and write a Core Word.

1. dove 1 | fish 4 | mile 2 | rows 3 | stem 2

2. curb 2 | leap 1 | grin 3 | bait 4 | quit 1

3. pipe 2 | into 1 | vote 3 | poem 4 | else 2

4. halo 4 | urge 3 | open 1 | slot 2 | thin 3

5. fast 3 | chin 3 | gift 2 | save 3 | loot 4

Search for Syllables Write the Core Word that contains the syllable underlined in each word below.

6. bu<u>zz</u>ard　　　8. pla<u>tt</u>er　　　10. tem<u>per</u>

7. ca<u>ttl</u>eman　　9. ma<u>ple</u>

Solve the Letter Puzzles Write the Core Word that fits each clue.

11. It has a *y*, an *m*, and a *t* but no *s*.
12. It has an *i*, an *l*, and a *b* but no *a*.
13. It has an *i*, a *g*, and an *l* but no *o*.
14. It has an *h*, a *t*, and an *i* but no *w*.
15. It has an *i*, a *t*, and an *m* but no *l*.

WRITE ON YOUR OWN

Write a description of a winter scene. Follow the Steps in the Writing Process on pages 134–135. Use at least four Core Words from this lesson in your description.

Prooofreding prakticee

a
c

1–5. Here is a draft of one student's description. Find five misspelled Core Words and write them correctly.

> After the december blizzerd, snow covered the ground like a soft, white kwilt. Our car looked like an igloo. The sudden stillness gave me a feeling of mistery. The only sound was the wristle of wind through the trees. Then I heard a shout. Our neighbor mr jabal had come to viset.

6–9. This student forgot to capitalize two proper nouns and an abbreviation and left out a punctuation mark. Copy the description and correct the errors.

Now proofread your own description and correct any errors.

CORE			CHALLENGE
quilt	limit	system	instinct
mystery	built	width	typical
glimpse	blizzard	simple	biscuit
igloo	whistle	visit	gymnast
myth	imitate	thrift	mischief

5 Spelling the Short *u* Sound

FOCUS

CORE

1. study
2. clumsy
3. trouble
4. trumpet
5. glove
6. hunger
7. thunder
8. country
9. bundle
10. none
11. bumblebee
12. honey
13. chuckle
14. money
15. struggle

CHALLENGE

16. justice
17. govern
18. customer
19. slumber
20. structure

Sound	Sign	Spelling		
short *u*	/u/	study	none	trouble

Say each word. Listen for the short *u* sound.

Study the spelling. How is the short *u* sound spelled in *study*, *none*, and *trouble*?

Write the words.

   1–9. Write the Core Words that have the short *u* sound spelled *u*.

   10–13. Write the Core Words that have the short *u* sound spelled *o*.

   14–15. Write the Core Words that have the short *u* sound spelled *ou*.

   16–20. Write the Challenge Words. Circle the letter that spells the short *u* sound in each word.

SPELLING TIP
The short *u* sound can be spelled *u*, *o*, or *ou*.

WORDS and MEANINGS

Write the Core Words that best complete the story.

Come to the Country

Every summer I visit my grandmother, who lives on a farm in the (1). In the morning the rooster sounds like a (2) waking us up. I smell breakfast cooking, and I can hardly control my (3). I eat pancakes until there are (4) left. Then I pack up a (5) of sandwiches for lunch and head outdoors. "Don't get into (6)!" Grandma says. I often stay out all day, unless I hear the rumble of (7).

I like to wander around the farm observing nature. For instance, did you ever see a (8) buzzing inside a flower? If you (9) the bee carefully, you can see it drinking the flower's nectar. Grandma raises honeybees. She makes (10) selling their (11).

In the evening Grandma may put on a baseball (12) and pitch a few balls to me. Or she might let me milk the cow. The first time I tried, I looked so funny that Grandma had to (13). My hands were so (14)! I really had quite a (15) before I got the knack of it.

Synonyms

Synonyms are words that have the same or nearly the same meaning. Write the Core Word that is a synonym for each word below.

16. nation
17. package
18. laugh

19. appetite
20. cash
21. zero

22. examine
23. battle
24. awkward

Break the Code Look at the code box. Each number or symbol represents a letter of a Core Word. Decode each group of numbers and symbols and write the Core Word you find.

Letter	a	b	c	d	e	f	g	h	i	j	k	l	m	n	o	p	q	r	s	t	u	v	w	x	y	z
Code	!	@	#	$	%	&	*	(	+	?	<	=	]	:	"	/	0	1	2	3	4	5	6	7	8	9

1. # = 4] 2 8
2. 2 3 1 4 * * = %
3. (4 : * % 1
4. @ 4 : $ = %
5. @ 4] @ = % @ % %
6. # " 4 : 3 1 8
7. 3 1 4] / % 3

Take Time to Rhyme Write the Core Word that creates a rhyme.

8. a friend you do homework with: a ___ buddy
9. bubblegum that gets stuck in your hair: bubble ___
10. a mistaken forecast of a storm: a ___ blunder
11. what a comedian earns: funny ___
12. what catchers feel for their mitts: ___ love
13. a funny hand trick: a knuckle ___
14. what a weak bee produces: runny ___
15. what a bad checkers player did: won ___

Use the Dictionary Words can have more than one meaning. Look up each underlined Core Word in your Speller Dictionary. Write the definition that shows how the word is used in the sentence.

16. There was a desk and chair in the study.
17. Those children hunger for attention.
18. She heard the thunder of a horse's hooves.
19. We moved from the city to the country.
20. It's so nice to see you, honey!

Imagine you have just come back from a visit. Write a thank-you note to your host or hostess. Follow the Steps in the Writing Process on pages 134–135 to write your note. Use at least four Core Words from this lesson.

Prooofreding prakticee

1–4. Here is a draft of part of a note that one student wrote. Find four misspelled Core Words and write them correctly.

> Dear Uncle Antoine,
>
> Thank you so much for having me as your guest. I hope I wasn't too much *truble*. It was wonderful to see the *contry* where I was born. Now I am saving all my money for my next trip. Also, I plan to *stoudy* French. Maybe I won't have to *strugle* so much with the language next time!

Now proofread your own note and correct any errors.

CORE			CHALLENGE
study	hunger	bumblebee	justice
clumsy	thunder	honey	govern
trouble	country	chuckle	customer
trumpet	bundle	money	slumber
glove	none	struggle	structure

Write a Core Word from Lesson 1 for each clue below. Each word you write will have at least two syllables and a short *a* sound.

1. You wash your hair with this.

2. This is a small house made of logs.

3. It covers you in bed.

4. Farmers use this machine in the field.

Write a Core Word from Lesson 2 to complete each sentence. The missing word will rhyme with the underlined word and have a short *e* sound.

5. Fixing the broken gate makes good <u>fence</u> ___ .

6. One should never rest in the ___ to find the <u>best</u>.

7. My aunt knits a <u>better</u> ___ .

8. With her straw broom, she <u>kept</u> the room well ___ .

Write each phrase or sentence below. Replace the underlined word or words with a Core Word from Lesson 3. Each word will have an /o/ or /ô/ sound. The new phrase or sentence is a famous quotation.

9. "There is no debt more lawful than the word of a just man nor anything which binds our actions more than a <u>vow</u>."
   — QUEEN ELIZABETH I OF ENGLAND

10. "I am not in the role of <u>ordinary</u> men."
    — WILLIAM SHAKESPEARE

11. "...a <u>wide</u> and ample road, whose dust is gold"
    — JOHN MILTON

12. "There is an <u>terrible</u> warmth about my heart."
    — JOHN KEATS

REVIEW

Write a Core Word from Lesson 4 that fits each group of words. Each word you write will have the short *i* sound.

13. house, snow, blocks, dome, ___
14. length, height, ___
15. clue, suspect, solution, ___
16. storm, wind, snow, ___

Write a Core Word from Lesson 5 to complete each sentence. The missing word will rhyme with the underlined word.

17. Dollars for a rabbit are <u>bunny</u> ___.
18. A mitten for a type of pigeon is a <u>dove</u> ___.
19. A friend to help you with your homework is a ___ <u>buddy</u>.
20. Twice as many problems are <u>double</u> ___.

7 Spelling the Long a and Long e Sounds

CORE

1. scrape
2. hasty
3. brief
4. favor
5. seize
6. danger
7. beaver
8. reindeer
9. retreat
10. reins
11. stale
12. sleigh
13. sleeves
14. great
15. praise

CHALLENGE

16. teammate
17. ache
18. relation
19. receive
20. maintain

FOCUS

Sound	Sign	Spelling			
long *a*	/ā/	stale	praise	great	sleigh
		reins	danger		
long *e*	/ē/	sleeves	brief	seize	retreat
		hasty			

Say each word. Listen for the long *a* and long *e* sounds.

Study the spelling. How is the /ā/ sound spelled in *stale, praise, great, sleigh, reins,* and *danger?* How is the /ē/ sound spelled in *sleeves, brief, seize, retreat,* and *hasty?*

Write the words.

1–15. Write the Core Words. Underline the letters that spell the /ā/ sound. Circle the letters that spell the /ē/ sound.

16–20. Write the Challenge Words. Circle the word that has both the /ā/ and /ē/ sounds.

SPELLING TIP

The long *a* sound can be spelled
a-e, ai, ea, eigh, ei, or *a.*
The long *e* sound can be spelled
ee, ie, ei, ea, or *y.*

WORDS and MEANINGS

Write the Core Words that best complete the story.

Working Animals

Beavers deserve __(1)__ for being such __(2)__ builders. You might think that beaver dams would last for only a __(3)__ period of time, but some actually last for years. Beavers work quickly but are never so __(4)__ as to do a poor job.

These animals look out for their friends, too. If they sense __(5)__, they do their pals a __(6)__ by slapping the water with their tails as a warning.

The beavers' main tools are their teeth. They use them to cut down trees and to cut off branches. Then they use their teeth and feet to __(7)__ the branches and drag them to the work site. They also use their teeth to peel and __(8)__ bark from trees. Bark is food for beavers. People might think it tastes __(9)__, but beavers love it.

Beavers are always ready to "roll up their __(10)__" and work, except during the winter. Then they __(11)__ into their dens. In pioneer days a winter traveler might have taken the __(12)__ of a horse-drawn __(13)__. This voyager was less likely to spot the antlers of a __(14)__ than the broad, flat tail of a __(15)__.

Homophones

Homophones are words that sound alike but have different spellings and meanings. Write the correct homophone to complete each sentence.

16. Please (great/grate) onions.
17. I feel (great/grate).
18. Ride the (sleigh/slay).
19. (Sleigh/Slay) the monster!
20. I hope it (reins/rains).
21. Hold the (reins/rains).

Lesson 7   25

Rhyme and Write
Each picture shows something that rhymes with a Core Word. Write the Core Words.

1. Rhymes with

2. Rhymes with

3. Rhymes with

4. Rhymes with

5. Rhymes with

Switch the Syllables
Each pair of words is divided into syllables. Take one syllable from each word to write a Core Word.

6. bea/con fe/ver
7. treat/ment re/play
8. sa/vor fa/mous
9. pret/ty has/ten
10. dan/dy gin/ger

Take a Close Look
Write Core Words to answer the questions.

11–12. Which two words begin with the same four letters?

13–14. Which two words use the same two letters, in a different order, to spell the long *e* sound?

15. From which spelling word could you drop the first letter to make a synonym for *lift*?

Write an adventure story that has a beaver as its main character. When you write, follow the writing process steps on pages 134–135. Use at least four Core Words from this lesson.

Prooofreding prakticee

1–5. Here is a draft of one student's story. Find five misspelled Core Words and write them correctly.

> A beever was trying to scrape some bark from a log. Suddenly, he sensed dainger. He looked up and saw a huge grizzly bear with grate big claws and teeth. For one breef moment, the beaver was too scared to move. Then he darted into the stream, just as the bear was about to sieze him.

Now proofread your own story and correct any errors.

CORE			CHALLENGE
scrape	danger	stale	teammate
hasty	beaver	sleigh	ache
brief	reindeer	sleeves	relation
favor	retreat	great	receive
seize	reins	praise	maintain

8 Spelling the Long *o* and Long *i* Sounds

CORE

1. quote
2. lightning
3. robot
4. boast
5. skyline
6. hotel
7. climate
8. growth
9. lifeboat
10. overgrown
11. stride
12. postpone
13. motor
14. idea
15. recite

CHALLENGE

16. typewriter
17. boulder
18. silence
19. although
20. ownership

Sound	Sign	Spelling		
long *o*	/ō/	quote	boast	growth
		motor		
long *i*	/ī/	climate	skyline	lightning

Say each word. Listen for the long *o* and long *i* sounds.

Study the spelling. How is the /ō/ sound spelled in *quote, boast, growth,* and *motor*? How is the /ī/ sound spelled in *climate, skyline,* and *lightning*?

Write the words.

1–15. Write the Core Words. Circle the letters that spell the /ō/ sound. Underline the letters that spell the /ī/ sound.

16–20. Write the Challenge Words. Circle the letters that spell the /ō/ sound. Underline the letters that spell the /ī/ sound.

SPELLING TIP

The long *o* sound can be spelled *o-e, oa, ow,* or *o*.
The long *i* sound can be spelled *i, y, i-e,* or *igh*.

28   Lesson 8

WORDS and MEANINGS

Write the Core Words that best complete the story.

A Frightful Boat Ride

"Okay, here's my story," the tourist told the reporter. "The morning was cloudy, but I had already rented a boat. So I didn't want to (1) my sailing trip because of the weather. The clerk at the (2) where I'm staying saw me (3) toward the dock and warned me of the storm. But did I listen? Oh, no! I said, 'Hey, I can handle it.' I had no (4) then what a silly (5) that was. I know now that although this (6) is mild, it can be tricky, too.

"No sooner had I set sail than the ripples became huge waves. Their sudden (7) told me I was in trouble. Suddenly (8) flashed! Then it got so dark I could hardly see the city (9) in the distance. I tried to work the sails, but I was moving as stiffly as a (10). Boy, did I wish my boat had a (11)! The boat and I were tossed around on the waves for quite a while. Finally, a passing ship saw me and sent out a (12) to save me.

"I guess I behaved like an (13) kid. I'd better study the rules for safe boating until I can (14) them from memory."

"Can I (15) you on that?" asked the reporter.

Compound Words

Compound words are made up of two or more smaller words. Join the words below to form compound words. Write the new words and a short definition of each one.

16. over + grown =

17. life + boat =

18. sky + line =

19. fire + fly =

20. back + bone =

Decode the Morse Code

Study the Morse code given in the box on the right. Then decode the groups of symbols below. Write each Core Word you find.

A ■■	B ■■■	C ■■■■	D ■■■
E ■	F ■■■■	G ■■■	H ■■■■
I ■■	J ■■■■	K ■■■	L ■■■■
M ■■	N ■■	O ■■■	P ■■■■
Q ■■■■	R ■■■	S ■■■	T ■
U ■■■	V ■■■■	W ■■■	X ■■■■
Y ■■■■	Z ■■■■		

1. ■■ ■■■ ■ ■■■ ■■■
2. ■■■■ ■■■ ■■ ■■■ ■■ ■■
3. ■■■■ ■■ ■■■ ■■■■ ■ ■■ ■■ ■■■
4. ■■■ ■■■ ■■■ ■ ■■ ■ ■■■■
5. ■■■ ■■■ ■■ ■ ■■■ ■■■ ■■■ ■
6. ■■■ ■■ ■■■ ■■■ ■■ ■■ ■
7. ■■■ ■ ■■■ ■■ ■ ■
8. ■■■■ ■■■ ■ ■■■
9. ■■■■ ■■ ■■■■ ■ ■■■ ■■■ ■■■ ■
10. ■■■ ■■■ ■■■■ ■■■ ■

Combine and Spell

One box contains all the vowels in a Core Word. The other contains all the consonants. Combine the letters to write each Core Word.

11. | oeo | vrgrwn |
12. | ie | strd |
13. | oa | bst |
14. | uoe | qt |
15. | iea | d |

Use the Dictionary

Write the Core Words you would find on a dictionary page with the guide words shown below. Write the words in the order you would find them.

16–18. furry/jabber

WRITE ON YOUR OWN

Write a diary entry that someone might write after a day on a boat. Use at least four Core Words from this lesson.

Proofreding prakticee

1-4. Here is the diary entry that one student wrote. Find four misspelled Core Words and write them correctly.

> July 15 1995—Today we left the hostel early and went on a boat trip to see whales. What a great ideea that was! The whales were totally amazing. our guide explained that they are mammals, even though they look like overgrone fish. I can't wait to bowst to Joshua that I've seen a real whale

5-7. This student forgot to capitalize one letter and left out a comma and a period. Copy the diary entry and correct the errors.

Now proofread your own diary entry and correct any errors.

CORE			CHALLENGE
quote	hotel	stride	typewriter
lightning	climate	postpone	boulder
robot	growth	motor	silence
boast	lifeboat	idea	although
skyline	overgrown	recite	ownership

9 Spelling the /ü/ and /ū/ Sounds

CORE

1. soup
2. usual
3. prove
4. unite
5. cruise
6. music
7. lunar
8. cartoon
9. clue
10. tissue
11. soothing
12. truth
13. noodle
14. scuba
15. smooth

CHALLENGE

16. junior
17. museum
18. routine
19. preview
20. nuisance

FOCUS

Sound	Sign	Spelling		
	/ü/	soup	prove	cruise
		clue	truth	smooth
long *u*	/ū/	music		

Say each word. Listen for the /ü/ and /ū/ sounds.

Study the spelling. How is the /ü/ sound spelled in *soup, prove, cruise, clue, truth,* and *smooth?* How is the /ū/ sound spelled in *music?*

Write the words.

1–15. Write the Core Words. Circle the letters that spell the /ü/ sound. Underline the letters that spell the /ū/ sound. One word has both sounds.

16–20. Write the Challenge Words. Circle the word that has the /ü/ sound spelled in another way. Underline the word that has the /ū/ sound spelled in another way.

SPELLING TIP
The /ü/ sound can be spelled *ou, o-e, ui-e, ue, u,* or *oo.*
The /ū/ sound can be spelled *u.*

WORDS and MEANINGS

Write the Core Words that best complete the story.

A Deep-Sea Adventure

Last summer I went on a sea (1) and went (2) diving. To tell you the (3), I didn't really want to go diving. I had to try it, though, to (4) that I wasn't scared.

I didn't have a (5) about how to begin, so the instructor helped me put on the mask, tank, and flippers. I felt like a creature from a (6) in the funny papers, but those are the (7) things that scuba divers wear. Then the instructor gave us some pointers, and before we knew it, we were jumping into the ocean.

At first the water was cloudy, and something (8) and slimy touched me. Yuck! It felt like a (9) in a bowl of chicken (10). But as we went deeper, the water grew clear. Then I actually started to enjoy myself. I began to feel like the astronauts must have felt when they walked on the (11) landscape. Being nearly weightless is such a nice, (12) feeling! The seaweed looked as delicate as green (13) paper, and the fish moved as if they were listening to peaceful (14). Swimming among them taught me how wonderful it can be to (15) with nature.

The Adverb Suffix -ly

You can change some adjectives to adverbs by adding the suffix -ly. Join these adjectives and -ly to write adverbs. Change a final y to i before adding -ly.

16. usual + ly =

17. soothing + ly =

18. smooth + ly =

19. clumsy + ly =

20. proper + ly =

21. common + ly =

22. prompt + ly =

23. hasty + ly =

24. awful + ly =

Search the Seashell
Follow the path from the opening of the seashell to its center. Find and write five Core Words.

1-5.

Change One or Add One
Study each word or name. Then change one letter or add one letter to make a Core Word. Write the Core Words.

6. soap
7. probe
8. Ruth
9. club
10. Cuba
11. unit
12. carton

Think and Write
Write the Core Word that completes each statement.

13. *Bumpy* is to *rough* as *flat* is to ___.
14. *Bathe* is to *washcloth* as *sneeze* is to ___.
15. *Shoe* is to *sneaker* as *pasta* is to ___.

How would you convince people to try the exciting sport of scuba diving? Write an ad for scuba diving lessons. Follow the writing process steps on pages 134–135 when you write your ad. Use at least four Core Words from this lesson.

Prooófreding prakticeé
a   c

1–4. Here is a draft of one student's ad. Find four misspelled Core Words and write them correctly.

> Are you tired of doing the usuel things on your vacation. This year, take a cruse with Diver Deb's School of Scuba Diving and enter the beautiful, suthing world of the sea. Each new sight will give you a cloo to the mysteries of the deep. What a thrill. Sign up now for the august class.

5–7. This student forgot to capitalize a proper noun and made two errors in end punctuation. Copy the ad and correct the errors.

Now proofread your own advertisement and correct any errors.

CORE			CHALLENGE
soup	music	soothing	junior
usual	lunar	truth	museum
prove	cartoon	noodle	routine
unite	clue	scuba	preview
cruise	tissue	smooth	nuisance

10 Spelling the /ûr/ Sound

CORE

1. burnt
2. churn
3. urban
4. occur
5. burden
6. hurdle
7. furnace
8. purpose
9. surplus
10. turkey
11. furnish
12. spurt
13. turmoil
14. splurge
15. current

FOCUS

Sound	Spelling
/ûr/	sp**ur**t

Say each word. Listen for the /ûr/ sound.

Study the spelling. How is the /ûr/ sound spelled in each word?

Write the words.

1–4. Write the Core Words that have one syllable. Circle the letters that spell the /ûr/ sound.

5–15. Write the Core Words that have two syllables. Circle the letters that spell the /ûr/ sound. Underline the word that has the /ûr/ sound in the *second* syllable.

16–20. Write the Challenge Words. Underline the three words that have the /ûr/ sound spelled in another way.

SPELLING TIP
The /ûr/ sound is often spelled *ur*.

CHALLENGE

16. journal
17. journey
18. surname
19. courtesy
20. surfboard

WORDS and MEANINGS

Write the Core Words that best complete the story.

From Turmoil to Turkey

The first year in America was hard on the Pilgrims. Nature forced them to jump over one (1) after another. The bitter winter was a heavy (2) to bear, and the Pilgrims could not grow or gather enough food. They had never dreamed that such hardships would (3) in their new land. Before long the Pilgrims were in a terrible state of (4).

Then some Native American neighbors offered to help. They took the time to (5) the Pilgrims with the skills they needed to survive. The natives taught the new arrivals to hunt, fish, and raise corn. In fact, the corn grew so well that it seemed to (6) from the soil. At harvest time the Pilgrims were amazed to find that they had produced more crops than they needed. They actually had a (7) of food! They decided to use the extra food to hold a feast. One (8) of the feast was to thank the Native Americans for their kindnesses.

In (9) times Americans on farms as well as in (10) areas still celebrate Thanksgiving. Today we no longer (11) our own butter, and we get our heat from a (12) rather than from a fire. But we still like to (13) on the biggest (14) we can fit in the oven—and hope it doesn't get (15)!

The Prefix re-

The prefix *re-* adds the meaning "again" to a word. For example, *refurnish* means "furnish again." Add *re-* to each word. Then write a short definition of the new word.

16. write   18. build   20. state

17. dial   19. hire

Words of a Feather
Write the Core Word that belongs with each group of turkey feathers.

1.  obstacle bar

2.  aim goal

3.  arise happen

4.  load weight

Search for Blends
Write a Core Word to answer each question.

5. Which word has the same beginning consonant blend as *split* and *splash?*
6. Which word has the same beginning consonants as *chair* and *cheap* and the same final consonants as *learn* and *thorn?*
7. Which word has the same beginning consonant blend as *space* and *sport* and the same final consonants as *apart* and *shirt?*
8. Which word has the same final consonants as *event* and *plant?*
9. Which word ends with three consonants?
10. Which word has the same final consonants as *finish* and *punish?*

Seek and Spell
Each small word below is hidden in a Core Word. Write the Core Words.

11. key
12. ban
13. plus
14. oil
15. ace

Use the Dictionary
Entry words are divided into syllables in the dictionary. Look up each Core Word below in your Speller Dictionary. Write each word and draw a line between the syllables.

16. occur
17. furnish
18. hurdle
19. furnace
20. burden

WRITE ON YOUR OWN

Write a short description of what life might have been like for early American settlers. Follow the writing process steps on pages 134–135 to write your description. Use at least four Core Words from this lesson.

Prooofreding prakticee

1–5. Here is a draft of one student's description. Find five misspelled Core Words and write them correctly.

> Life for the early settlers was often filled with tourmoil. Sometimes forest fires would occur, and the homes of the settlers would be birnt. Sometimes the settlers could not grow a sirplus of crops, so they could not save any food for winter. But their strong sense of perpose helped them bear each birden.

Now proofread your own description and correct any errors.

CORE			CHALLENGE
burnt	hurdle	furnish	journal
churn	furnace	spurt	journey
urban	purpose	turmoil	surname
occur	surplus	splurge	courtesy
burden	turkey	current	surfboard

11 Easily Misspelled Words

CORE

1. syrup
2. lose
3. diary
4. corps
5. busy
6. dozen
7. recipe
8. angel
9. tongue
10. beige
11. angle
12. separate
13. machine
14. business
15. honor

CHALLENGE

16. chord
17. onion
18. soldier
19. sheriff
20. sergeant

Words and Meanings

Write the Core Words that best complete the story.

The Business of Cooking

Cooking is a skill that everyone should learn. Good food not only delights the (1), but it warms the heart as well. We all feel great when we can serve our guests of (2) something tasty.

Cooking is easy, too. Many cookbooks start with the basics. For example, they explain how to (3) the yolk from the white of an egg. They show you how to hold a spoon at just the right (4) for beating. They even tell you how to keep raw, peeled potatoes from turning a (5) color. Do you think you are too (6) to spend time cooking? Well, today's cookbooks suggest that you save time by using a (7) such as a food processor.

Start by making something simple, like pancakes with (8). Follow the cookbook's (9) carefully, and use a bookmark so you won't (10) your place. Then try something fancier, like an (11) food cake. You might want to record your successes and failures in a (12).

When you make your first complete meal, don't try to prepare a (13) different dishes. And keep your guest list short, too. Don't invite an army (14) to your first dinner! Someday, though, you may become a really good cook. If you want to feed a lot of people then begin your own restaurant or food (15).

The Endings -er and -est

Add -er to an adjective below if it is comparing two things. Add -est if the adjective is comparing three or more things. Remember to change a final y to i before adding the ending.

16. a (busy) day than Monday
17. the (tall) tree in the forest
18. the (fluffy) kitten in the city
19. a (new) bike than mine
20. the (pretty) shell on the beach

Wise Words

Write a Core Word to complete the wise saying in each fortune cookie.

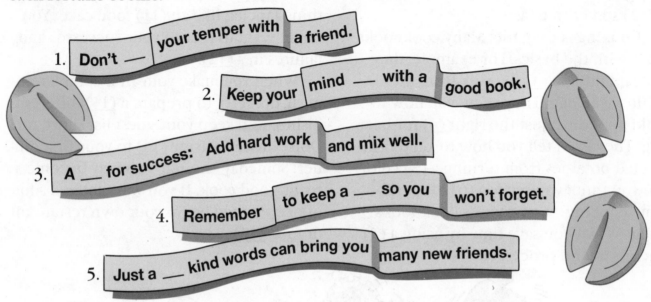

1. Don't — your temper with a friend.
2. Keep your mind — with a good book.
3. A — for success: Add hard work and mix well.
4. Remember to keep a — so you won't forget.
5. Just a — kind words can bring you many new friends.

Get to the Core

Write a Core Word to answer each question.

6. Which Core Word ends with two silent consonants?
7. Which Core Word ends with two silent vowels?
8. Which Core Word begins with a silent consonant?
9. Which Core Word uses another Core Word as its base word?
10–11. Which two Core Words have exactly the same letters?

Subtract and Spell

Subtract the word shown from each group of letters. Write the Core Word that remains.

12. bceraigyeon – crayon =
13. fseopalrlatoew – follow =
14. wsafyfrulpe – waffle =
15. msaewcihinnge – sewing =

WRITE ON YOUR OWN

Write a set of directions for making something good to eat. To write your directions, follow the writing process steps on pages 134–135. Use at least four Core Words from this lesson.

Prooofreding prakticee
a c

1-4. Here is a draft of one student's set of directions. Find four misspelled Core Words and write them correctly.

> This is a good recipy for a bisy host or hostess who wants to serve a great party snack. Start with a duzen hard-boiled eggs. Peel them, slice them in half, and seperate the yolks from the whites. Mash the yolks and mix them with mayonnaise. Then put some of the mixture in each egg white.

Now proofread your own set of directions and correct any errors.

CORE			CHALLENGE
syrup	dozen	angle	chord
lose	recipe	separate	onion
diary	angel	machine	soldier
corps	tongue	business	sheriff
busy	beige	honor	sergeant

12 REVIEW

Write a Core Word from Lesson 7 for each clue below. Each word will have a long *a* sound or a long *e* sound.

1. Red-nosed Rudolph was one of these.
2. These cover your arms.
3. An army does this when it is losing.
4. This is another word for terrific.

Write a Core Word from Lesson 8 to complete each sentence. The missing word will rhyme with the underlined word and have a long *o* sound or a long *i* sound.

5. "Baaa... Baaa..." is a <u>goat</u> ___.
6. A long step to your left or right might be called a <u>side</u> ___.
7. Someone with an engine on the water is probably a ___ <u>boater</u>.
8. The button near the inn's door is a ___ <u>doorbell</u>.

Write a Core Word from Lesson 9 that means the opposite of each word below. Each word you write will have a /ü/ or a /ū/ sound.

9. a lie
10. rough
11. divide
12. uncommon

Write each phrase or sentence below. Replace the underlined word or words with a Core Word from Lesson 10. Each word will have a /ûr/ sound. The corrected phrase or sentence is a famous quotation.

13. "And ever those, who would
     enjoyment gain
     Must find it in the goal
        they pursue." — SARAH JOSEPHA HALE

14. "The feathered animal often eaten at
     Thanksgiving is a much more respectable
     bird." — BENJAMIN FRANKLIN

15. "The emptiness of ages in his face,
     And on his back, the weight
     of the world." — EDWIN MARKHAM

16. "Time is a sort of river of passing events,
     and strong is its flowing tide." — MARCUS AURELIUS

Write a Core Word from Lesson 11 that fits each group of words.

17. lips, teeth, gums, ___

18. tan, white, brown, cream, ___

19. pancakes, waffles, French toast, ___

20. cookbook, directions, spices, ___

13 Spelling Consonant Blends

CORE

1. cruel
2. throat
3. greedy
4. swallow
5. broken
6. stubborn
7. clinic
8. stumble
9. clothing
10. steeple
11. clover
12. startle
13. blister
14. sparkle
15. flavor

CHALLENGE

16. drizzle
17. crystal
18. classify
19. blueprint
20. strength

FOCUS

Say each word. Listen for the consonant sounds at the beginning of each word. Two or more consonants that are pronounced together are called a consonant blend.

Study the spelling. What three consonants does *throat* begin with? What two consonants does *swallow* begin with?

Write the words.

1–15. Write the Core Words. Circle the two or three-letter consonant blend that begins each word.

16–20. Write the Challenge Words. Circle the consonant blend that begins each word.

SPELLING TIP

Many words begin with the consonant blends *cr, fl, sp, gr, br, cl, bl, st, sw,* and *thr.*

WORDS and MEANINGS

Write the Core Words that best complete the story.

A Stubborn Burro

Maria is going to the market to sell the shirts and other (1) her mother has made. Then she will pick up some medicine at the (2) to help heal her father's (3) leg. She ties the sack of clothing onto the back of her little burro, Pepe. She then makes sure the load is not so heavy that it will make him (4) and fall. She checks the rope as well to make sure it won't rub Pepe's skin and cause a (5). Meanwhile, she daydreams about the day ahead.

Suddenly, the bells in the church (6) ring. They (7) Maria from her daydream and remind her that she needs to hurry. But Pepe refuses to hurry. As usual he is being (8). Seeing the nearby stream (9) in the sunshine makes his (10) feel dry. He looks at Maria, and his eyes seem to say, "How could you be so (11) to your dear little Pepe!" Maria laughs and lets him take a (12) of water. Then she grabs a handful of fresh, green (13), because she knows Pepe is (14) for its sweet (15). Eating from her hand, the little burro follows her down the mountain.

The Suffix -ful

The suffix -ful means "full of." *Flavorful* means "full of flavor." Write a word that ends with -ful and means the same as each phrase below.

16. full of peace
17. full of power
18. full of joy

19. full of stress
20. full of color
21. full of hope

22. full of pain
23. full of success
24. full of delight

Search and Stack Each burro can carry three words stacked on its back, but they must be in alphabetical order. Write the Core Word that goes in alphabetical order between the other two words.

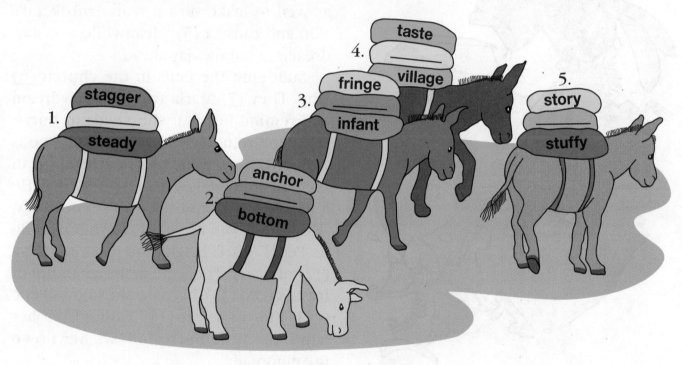

Leap and Write Replace each letter below with the next letter of the alphabet to write five Core Words. For example, replace *a* with *b*, *b* with *c*, and so on.

6. aqnjdm   7. bknsghmf   8. bknudq   9. rsddokd   10. bkhmhb

Use the Dictionary Write the entry word that you would look up in a dictionary to find each word below.

11. flavorful   12. swallowing   13. stumbled   14. cruelest   15. sparkles

Think of an animal that you have or would like to have as a pet. Write a list of do's and don't's on how to care for this pet. Use at least four Core Words from this lesson.

Prooofreding prakticee
a c

1-4. Here's a list of pet-care rules that one student wrote. Find four misspelled words and write them correctly.

1. Watch what your dog eats Dogs can be greedy!
2. A dog's collar must not be too tight around the throte.
3. If your dog is ill, take it to an Animal klinic.
4. Dogs need love, don't let its heart be brokan.
5. Above all, never be crewl to your dog in any way.

5-7. The student who wrote this list of rules left out one end punctuation mark and forgot to capitalize one letter. She also capitalized one letter that should not be capitalized. Make a copy of the list and correct the errors.

Now proofread your own list of rules and correct any errors.

CORE			CHALLENGE
cruel	stubborn	clover	drizzle
throat	clinic	startle	crystal
greedy	stumble	blister	classify
swallow	clothing	sparkle	blueprint
broken	steeple	flavor	strength

14 Spelling the /ou/ Sound

CORE

1. hour
2. however
3. pouch
4. coward
5. crouch
6. powder
7. blouse
8. shower
9. amount
10. towel
11. outward
12. browse
13. thousand
14. pronounce
15. account

CHALLENGE

16. bough
17. bloodhound
18. astounding
19. chowder
20. allowance

FOCUS

Sound	Spelling	
/ou/	hour	browse

Say each word. Listen for the vowel sound in *hour* and *coward*.

Study the spelling. How is the /ou/ sound spelled in *hour?* How is it spelled in *coward?*

Write the words.

1–9. Write the Core Words that have the /ou/ sound spelled *ou*.

10–15. Write the Core Words that have the /ou/ sound spelled *ow*.

16–20. Write the Challenge Words. Circle the letters that spell the /ou/ sound. Hint: One Challenge Word has the /ou/ sound spelled with four letters.

SPELLING TIP
The /ou/ sound is often spelled *ou* or *ow.*

WORDS and MEANINGS

Write the Core Words that best complete the story.

Shopping Around

When the phone rang, I ran dripping wet from the (1), grabbed a bath (2) from the rack, and picked up the receiver. It was Sue, inviting me to go shopping with her. "I'll be ready in an (3)," I said.

When Sue and I go shopping, I usually just (4). Sue, (5), is a serious shopper. That day, our first stop was a toy store. Sue bought her little brother a stuffed kangaroo with a joey in its (6). The next stop was a clothing store, where Sue bought a silk (7). I thought it was ugly, but I was too much of a (8) to say so.

Then we went to a cosmetic store. Sue bought some face (9) and some perfume whose name was impossible to (10). By this time I was getting tired, but Sue showed no (11) signs of slowing down. Soon we were in a jewelry store. I began to get nervous when I saw Sue (12) down in front of the showcase to study the diamond earrings. "Sue," I said, "those cost almost a (13) dollars! That's a huge (14) of money!"

"I know," said Sue. "It's a good thing I have a charge (15)!"

The Suffix -ward

The suffix **-ward** means "moving or happening in the direction of." *Outward* means "moving out or away from." Write a word with the suffix **-ward** that means the same as each phrase below.

16. moving up
17. moving in
18. happening after

19. moving east
20. moving west
21. moving north

22. moving south
23. moving toward the sky
24. moving toward the earth
25. moving to the side

Solve the Puzzles Match the puzzle parts and spell four Core Words.

1. | pow | ard |

3. | tow | mount |

2. | cow | el |

4. | a | der |

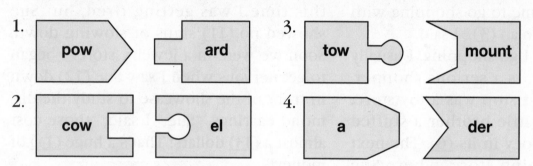

Get the Message Fill in the missing letters and write a Core Word.
Then use the letters that belong above the dollar signs to write a two-word message to shoppers.

5. b _ _ w _ e
    $

8. _ o w _ _
    $

11. _ u t _ a _ d
     $

6. _ c _ o _ n _
    $

9. _ r o _ o _ n _ _
    $

12. Write the message
     to shoppers.

7. _ o w e _ e _
    $

10. c _ _ u c _
     $

Think and Write Write the Core Word that fits each clue.

13. The little hand points to it.
14. It's the opposite of *hero*.
15. It has ruined many picnics.
16. It gets wet as it dries.
17. It comes after 999.
18. It has an *ouch* in it, but no consonant blend.
19. It starts with a consonant blend and rhymes with *mouse*.
20. It's a compound word.

Think of a place where you like to shop. Then follow the Steps in the Writing Process on pages 134–135 to write a description of this place. See if you can make your reader see why you like to shop there. Use at least four Core Words from this lesson.

Prooofreding prakticee

1–5. Here's a draft of the description that one student wrote. Find five misspelled words and write them correctly.

> Harvees is a huge store. However, you don't need a huge amownt of money to shop there. The store has a thousand different departments, where you can bruy anything from a blowse to a beach touel. There's even a lunch counter. It's fun to spend an howr there with a friend just to brouse.

Now proofread your description and correct any errors.

CORE			CHALLENGE
hour	powder	outward	bough
however	blouse	browse	bloodhound
pouch	shower	thousand	astounding
coward	amount	pronounce	chowder
crouch	towel	account	allowance

15 Spelling the Final /əl/ Sound

CORE

1. title
2. mammal
3. barrel
4. sandal
5. stable
6. marvel
7. middle
8. local
9. waffle
10. trial
11. level
12. metal
13. model
14. signal
15. cable

CHALLENGE

16. grumble
17. several
18. label
19. missile
20. tremble

FOCUS

Sound	Spelling		
/əl/	title	barrel	mammal

Say each word. Listen for the final /əl/ sound you hear in *title*, *barrel*, and *mammal*.

Study the spelling. How is the /əl/ sound spelled in *title?* How is it spelled in *barrel* and in *mammal?*

Write the words.

1–5. Write the Core Words that have the final /əl/ sound spelled *le*.

6–11. Write the Core Words that have the final /əl/ sound spelled *al*.

12–15. Write the Core Words that have the final/əl/ sound spelled *el*.

16–20. Write the Challenge Words. Circle the letters that spell the final /əl/ sound. Hint: One Challenge Word has the /əl/ sound spelled with three letters.

SPELLING TIP

The /əl/ sound may be spelled *le, al,* or *el*.

WORDS and MEANINGS

Write the Core Words that best complete the story.

What's on Cable?

When you think of what an amazing invention television is, you can't help but (1)! TV stations transmit an electrical (2) that travels to your TV set. You can watch a program produced by your (3) community station or one that is broadcast from far away. If you want to pay extra, you can watch additional TV stations that are brought to your home through an underground (4).

Some programs are educational, such as one whose (5) is "World of Wonder." On this show, you might learn how a certain kind of (6) feeds its young or how people first made tools out of (7). A cooking show might teach you how to make a (8) or how to be sure meat is cooked in the (9). A home repair show might demonstrate how to make a tilted floor (10) or a wobbly chair (11).

Most shows are mainly for fun. A home-shopping station might show a fashion (12) wearing a new kind of (13). In one children's show, a large puppet lives inside a trash (14). And adults love to watch TV lawyers show their skill in court during a (15).

The Suffix -al

The -al suffix changes a noun to an adjective. It adds the meaning "of" to the word. *Season* + *al* becomes *seasonal*, "of a season or seasons." Make adjectives of these words by adding -al. You may have to change the endings of some words first.

16. person
17. clinic
18. coast
19. nature
20. music
21. magic
22. nation
23. globe
24. family

Word Play

Tune In and Spell The contestants on this game show are given spelling clues. Help them win by writing the Core Word that fits each clue.

1. Change one letter and this word becomes *baffle*.
2. Take away one letter and this word becomes *table*.
3. *Camel* is an example of this word and also rhymes with it.
4. This word is the base word of *marvelous*.
5. The base word of this word is *try*.
6. This word has the same last four letters as *paddle*.
7. This word rhymes with another Core Word but is shorter.
8. This word begins like *sanitary* and ends like *tidal*.
9. The first syllable of this word rhymes with *wear*.
10. The first syllable has a long *o* sound.

Listen and Write Write two Core Words that have the vowel sound you hear in each word below.

11. cry
12. hot

13. men
14. sit

15. tail

Use the Dictionary Look up each of the following words in your Speller Dictionary. Write each part of speech that the word can be.

16. marvel
17. stable

18. mammal
19. middle

20. model

WRITE ON YOUR OWN

AMAZING INVENTIONS

Follow the Steps in the Writing Process on pages 134–135 to write a script for a TV show. Create your own characters or use characters from a real TV show. Include at least four Core Words.

Proofreding prakticee

1–4. Here's a draft of the script that one student wrote. Find four misspelled words and write them correctly.

ASTRONAUT: this planet is a marvel! Look at this rock, Captain perez. It contains some strange kind of metle.

CAPTAIN: You can explore the local area as long as you stay where the ground is leval. Be careful, though? If your cabel snaps, you will have no way to signel the crew

5–8. The student who wrote this script made two mistakes in end punctuation and forgot to capitalize two letters. Copy this script and correct the errors.

Now proofread your own script and correct any errors.

CORE			CHALLENGE
title	marvel	level	grumble
mammal	middle	metal	several
barrel	local	model	label
sandal	waffle	signal	missile
stable	trial	cable	tremble

16 Spelling the /ôr/ and /är/ Sounds

CORE

1. pour
2. parcel
3. warm
4. target
5. force
6. normal
7. orbit
8. carpet
9. adore
10. artist
11. afford
12. starve
13. mortal
14. doorbell
15. market

CHALLENGE

16. barbecue
17. porcupine
18. courtyard
19. argument
20. corral

Sound	Spelling
/ôr/	pour warm force doorbell
/är/	parcel

Say each word. Listen for the vowel plus /r/ sound in *pour*. Listen for the vowel plus /r/ sound in *parcel*.

Study the spelling. How is the /ôr/ sound spelled in *pour, warm, force,* and *doorbell?* How is the /är/ sound spelled in *parcel?*

Write the words.

1–15. Write the Core Words. Circle the letters that spell the vowel plus /r/ sound in each word.

16–20. Write the Challenge Words. Circle the letters that spell the vowel plus /r/ sound in each word.

SPELLING TIP

The /ôr/ sound may be spelled *our, ar, or,* or *oor.* The /är/ sound is often spelled *ar.*

WORDS and MEANINGS

Write the Core Words that best complete the story.

Carnival Glory

Long ago, a carnival came to my town during the (1) days of summer. Like any (2) little girl, I used to (3) going to the carnival. No one had to (4) me to wake up on carnival day. I was always ready to go as soon as my friend Emily rang the (5).

At the carnival we rode the Ferris wheel, circling like a planet in its (6). Then we went to see the magician. Outside his tent was a picture of him. He was sitting on a flying (7) that looked just like the rug in my front hall. In another tent a man ate fire and swallowed knives.

I was sure he would receive a (8) wound, but he never got hurt. We paid a nickel to throw darts at a (9). Then we watched an (10) drawing the portrait of anyone who could (11) to pay fifty cents.

By noon we were so hungry we thought we would (12). Part of the carnival was an outdoor (13) where we stopped to buy some food. We watched a vendor (14) cups of cider from a jug and wrap up some little meat pies for us. Then we carried our (15) to a shady tree and had a picnic.

The Prefix *en-*

The prefix *en-* means "to make" or "to cause to be." *Enforce* means "to cause to be in force." Write a word with the prefix *en-* that means the same as each phrase below.

16. to cause danger to
17. to make able
18. to make into a slave

19. to make large
20. to cause to be in a trap
21. to make rich

22. to make sure
23. to make a circle around
24. to cause to be in a tangle

Lesson 16   59

Spin the Syllables Match the syllables to write Core Words.

1–7. If you could make the lucky spin, seven Core Words would appear on the wheel of fortune. Write the Core Words.

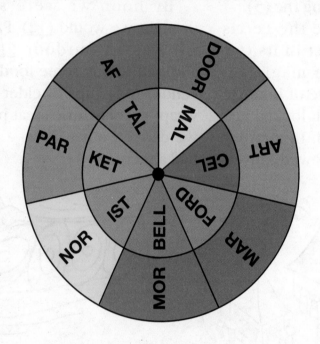

Rhyme and Respond Complete each answer with a rhyming Core Word.

8. Q: What do you do when the turkey comes out of the oven?
   A: carve or ___

9. Q: What do you do when you finish your juice but are still thirsty?
   A: ___ more

10. Q: What do you call a hurricane on a hot day? A: a ___ storm

11. Q: What's another way of saying "pony power"? A: horse ___

Combine and Write Combine little words to write Core Words.

12–15. Combine pairs of the little words below to write four Core Words.

get   bit   pet   ore   tar   ad   car   or

A memoir is a memory that someone puts into writing. Follow the Steps in the Writing Process on pages 134–135 to write a memoir about an experience you had at a carnival, an amusement park, a parade, a picnic, or a party. Use at least four Core Words from this lesson.

Prooofreding prakticee

1–5. Here's a draft of the memoir that one student wrote. Find five misspelled words and write them correctly.

> My sister said I would ador the roller coaster, so I tried it. From the minute the cars began to move, I was sure I was in mourtal danger. And even when the ride was over, my head kept spinning as if I was in orebit. My sister said that was nourmal, but I was glad we couldn't affoord to go again.

Now proofread your own memoir and correct any errors.

CORE			CHALLENGE
pour	normal	afford	barbecue
parcel	orbit	starve	porcupine
warm	carpet	mortal	courtyard
target	adore	doorbell	argument
force	artist	market	corral

17 Spelling Homophones

CORE

1. real
2. reel
3. tide
4. tied
5. horse
6. hoarse
7. plane
8. plain
9. break
10. brake
11. throne
12. thrown
13. petal
14. pedal
15. peddle

FOCUS

Say each word. Listen for words that sound the same or nearly the same but are spelled differently.

Study the spelling. What is a *break?* What is a *brake?* What is the difference in the spelling of *break* and *brake?*

Write the words.

1–15. Write the Core Words in homophone groups. Circle the homophones with two syllables.

16–20. Write the Challenge Words. Circle the word that is a homophone for *muscles.*

SPELLING TIP
Some words sound the same or nearly the same but have different spellings and meanings.

CHALLENGE

16. wade
17. weighed
18. weather
19. whether
20. mussels

WORDS and MEANINGS

Write the Core Words that best complete the story.

From Throne to Thrown

One day the king got up from his (1)
And went out to ride his (2) alone,
Out by the sea where the (3) flows
And air is fresh as the (4) of a rose.
Suddenly the king was (5) to the sand;
He tried to get up but couldn't stand.
His horse ran away. (It wasn't (6).)
"Now I'm lost," the poor king sighed.
His calls for help were all in vain–the sea
was as loud as a low–flying (7).
His voice grew too (8) to be heard
By anyone but a clam or a bird.
Now, a boy on a bike passed by
With a rod and (9) and fish to fry.
The boy said, "Can this really be?"

He put on his (10) and stopped to see.
He said, "Oh King, your leg must ache!
You're lucky that it didn't (11).
It's (12) that you should be in bed.
You'll ride my handlebars," he said.
The boy helped the king onto his bike
And headed for the main turnpike.
With a foot on each (13) he rode fast,
Until they reached the castle at last.
The king said, "Thanks for the lift.
Here's a (14) gold medal as a gift."
The boy said, "Thank you for the medal
And now I have some fish to (15)."

The Suffix -ity

The suffix -ity means "the quality of being."
The word *reality* means "the quality of
being real." Write a word with the suffix -ity
that means the same as each phrase below.

16. quality of being popular
17. quality of being solid
18. quality of being final

19. quality of being mortal
20. quality of being similar
21. quality of being general

22. quality of being normal
23. quality of being brutal
24. quality of being original

Flag the Right Word

If a word appears on a white banner, write a Core Word that is a synonym for the word. If a word appears on a colored banner, write a Core Word that is an antonym for the word.

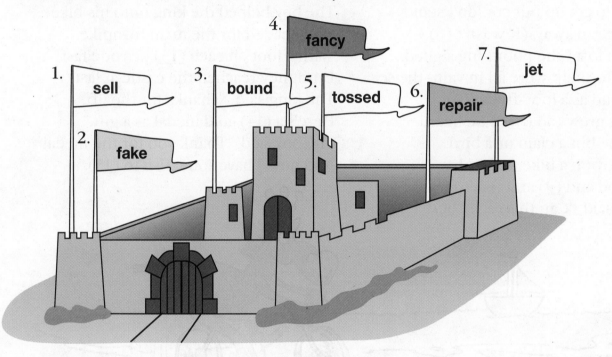

1. sell
2. fake
3. bound
4. fancy
5. tossed
6. repair
7. jet

Think and Write

Write the Core Word that matches each clue.

8. It has one *t* and the /əl/ sound.
9. It has the /ī/ sound and is a noun.
10. It has two syllables and one *d*.
11. It begins with three consonants and has an *e*.
12. It has the /ē/ sound and no *a*.

Use the Dictionary

Each dictionary pronunciation below shows how two Core Words are pronounced. Write the Core Words.

13. /hôrs/   14. /rēl/   15. /ped ′ əl/   16. /brāk/

Write a poem that tells a story about a brave or kind deed. Follow the Steps in the Writing Process on pages 134-135 to write your poem. Use at least four Core Words from this lesson.

Prooofreding prakticee

1-5. Here is the draft of a poem that one student wrote. Find five misspelled words and write them correctly.

A girl was watching the waves brake as the tide went slowly out. "Help! Help me! Please!" she heard a horse voice shout.
A boy in a boat had lost his oar. It was plane he could not swim. The girl found a rope and quickly threw one end of it to him.
He grabbed the rope she had throne and held on like never before. By pulling and pulling, she was able to real him in to shore.

Now proofread your own poem and correct any errors.

CORE			CHALLENGE
real	hoarse	throne	wade
reel	plane	thrown	weighed
tide	plain	petal	weather
tied	break	pedal	whether
horse	brake	peddle	mussels

Write a Core Word from Lesson 13 to complete each sentence. The missing word will rhyme with the underlined word and begin with *thr*, *fl*, *cl*, or *br*.

1. A neck sweater could be called a ___ ____ coat.
2. A refrigerator is ___ ____ saver.
3. Someone who wanders over the grass is a ___ ____ rover.
4. A split coin is a ___ ____ token.

Write a Core Word from Lesson 14 that means the same as the word or phrase below. Each word will have an /ou/ sound.

5. to sound a word by syllables
6. sixty minutes
7. a short rain or a way of bathing
8. a slow, casual look

Write a Core Word from Lesson 15 that fits each clue below. Each word will have an /əl/ sound.

9. A dog, a whale, or a human is an example.
10. It is a kind of home for horses.
11. You always find this the same distance from two sides.
12. It is found on a foot in warm weather.

Write each sentence or phrase below. Replace the underlined word or words with a Core Word from Lesson 16. Each word will have an /ôr/ or an /är/ sound. The corrected phrase or sentence is a famous quotation.

13. "Just then, with a wink and a sly <u>regular or usual</u> lurch,
The owl, very gravely, got down from his perch."

    —*James Thomas Fields*

14. "I may command where I <u>love</u>." — *William Shakespeare*

15. "We cannot remember that we are <u>subject to death</u>, and that we have one day to leave all things behind us."

    — *Giulia Gonzaga*

16. "We must grant the <u>creative person</u> his subject."

    —*Henry James*

Write a Core Word from Lesson 17 that means the opposite of each word below. Each word will have a homophone. Be sure you choose the correct meaning and spelling.

17. fake
18. fix
19. unclear and complicated
20. loosened

19 Spelling Words With -ed or -ing

CORE

1. waited
2. tracing
3. wagged
4. followed
5. handling
6. planned
7. paying
8. stepping
9. hanging
10. shopping
11. crawling
12. dropped
13. gardening
14. weeding
15. whispering

CHALLENGE

16. battling
17. choosing
18. remembered
19. meddling
20. referring

FOCUS

Say each word. Listen for the **-ed** and **-ing** endings.

Study the spelling. What letter in *plan* was doubled when **-ed** was added? What letter in *trace* was dropped when **-ing** was added?

Write the words.

1–15. Write the Core Words. Underline the words in which a final consonant was doubled when **-ed** or **-ing** was added. Circle the words in which a final *e* was dropped when **-ing** was added.

16–20. Write the Challenge Words. Underline the word in which a final consonant was doubled when **-ing** was added. Circle the words in which a final *e* was dropped when **-ing** was added.

SPELLING TIP

Words that end with a single vowel and a single consonant often double the final consonant when **-ed** or **-ing** is added. Words that end with *e* often drop the *e* when **-ed** or **-ing** is added.

Write the Core Words that best complete the story.

The Joy of Gardening

I had (1) eagerly for spring to come. Because (2) is my favorite hobby, I had already (3) what I would grow in my garden. And now, finally, spring was here!

First, I went (4) to buy seeds. After (5) $5.00 for several packets, I went home to pull weeds. For me (6) is the only unpleasant part of gardening. I don't like (7) around on my hands and knees, and I don't enjoy (8) the worms that sometimes come up with the weeds.

After weeding I used a sharp stick to make a series of grooves in the soil, (9) the pattern I had made last spring. I (10) the seeds into the grooves, walking carefully to keep from (11) on the seeds. Then I covered the seeds with soil. Soon, I thought, these seeds will be plants with beautiful blossoms (12) from their stems! Even my dog, Matty, (13) her tail with excitement.

The sky had turned gray, and the trees began to make a (14) sound. In moments the first raindrops began to fall. What luck! Now I wouldn't have to water the garden! I headed for cover, and Matty (15) close behind.

The Ending -er

The ending -er means "one who ___." For example, *shopper* means "one who shops." Write a definition of each word below. Begin your definition with "one who."

16. waiter
17. follower
18. payer
19. handler
20. gardener
21. planner
22. peddler
23. loser
24. biker

Solve the Puzzle Write the two Core Words that would fit in each puzzle.

1–8.

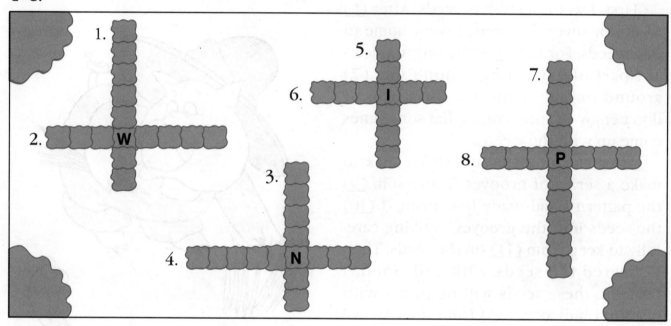

Search and Spell One part of each compound word below is also part of a Core Word. Write the Core Word.

9. handlebars
10. wagonload
11. ragweed
12. footstep
13. workshop
14. payroll
15. hangnail

Write the Rhyme Write the Core Word that completes each rhyme.

16. When ice is hardening,
    It is no time for ___.
17. When the rain stops falling,
    The worms start ___.
18. When her first bite was swallowed,
    Her next bite ___.
19. When you do too much erasing,
    You are better off ___.
20. When your buttons start popping,
    It is time to go ___.

70   Lesson 19

WRITE ON YOUR OWN

Write a funny story about a worm in a garden. Follow the writing process steps on pages 134–135 to write your story. Use at least four Core Words from this lesson.

Prooofreding prakticee

1–5. Here is a draft of one student's story. Find five misspelled Core Words and write them correctly.

> I was hangging around in my tunnel when some earth droped from my ceiling. Crawlling out my front door, I saw that a giant was gardening on my roof. I had not planed on this, so I waitted until the giant was not paying attention. Then I followed his footsteps and ate each seed that he planted.

Now proofread your own story and correct any errors.

CORE			CHALLENGE
waited	planned	crawling	battling
tracing	paying	dropped	choosing
wagged	stepping	gardening	remembered
followed	hanging	weeding	meddling
handling	shopping	whispering	referring

20 Spelling More Plurals

CORE

1. potato
2. potatoes
3. zero
4. zeros
5. tomato
6. tomatoes
7. piano
8. pianos
9. hero
10. heroes
11. radio
12. radios
13. echo
14. echoes
15. mosquitoes

FOCUS

Say the words. Listen for the singular or plural ending of each word.

Study the spelling. What letters are added to *potato* to make it plural? What letter is added to *zero* to make it plural?

Write the words.

1–7. Write the singular Core Words.

8–15. Write the plural Core Words. Circle the words that end in **-es**.

16–20. Write the Challenge Words. Underline the three words that have singular forms that end with the long *o* sound. Circle the letter in those words that was added to form the plural.

SPELLING TIP
The plural of words ending in *o* is formed by adding **-s** or **-es**.

CHALLENGE

16. studios
17. centuries
18. rodeos
19. glossaries
20. dynamos

Words and Meanings

Write the Core Words that best complete the story.

For the Love of Music

I am a music lover, and all of my (1) are famous musicians. One day I heard a great pianist on a (2) program, and he became my biggest (3). After I heard him play,

each note came back to me like an (4). Listening to these (5), I pretended that I was the one playing and people everywhere were tuning in their (6) to hear me.

I decided I wanted to take (7) lessons, but my mother said (8) were too expensive. So I began to study the violin. However, it turned out that I had no talent for the violin. My teacher, who usually graded on a scale of one to five, gave me a (9). She also mentioned that in her twenty-five years of teaching, she had given only two other (10). I can't blame her, really. My playing sounded like (11) do when they buzz your ears.

Before I was to give my first recital, I dreamed that someone in the audience threw a juicy, red (12) and a mashed (13) at me. The next day I quit taking violin lessons. It's not that I don't like juicy (14) or mashed (15). I would just rather have them for dinner than in my hair!

The Suffix -ic

The suffix -ic means "having to do with" or "like." For example, heroic means "like a hero." Write a word for each definition below. Each word will have the -ic suffix.

16. having to do with history
17. like a cube
18. like a magnet

19. like an artist
20. like an angel
21. like a melody

22. having to do with oceans
23. having to do with climate
24. having to do with tragedy

Take Note! Figure out the missing letters and write the Core Words. Then use the letters that would go above the musical notes to write the answer to question 10.

1. _ _ d _ _ _

2. _ _ a _ _

3. r _ _ _ _

4. _ _ h _ _ _

5. z _ _ _

6. _ _ t _ _ _ _

7. _ o _ _ _ t _ _ _

8. _ _ a _ _

9. _ _ m _ _ _ _ _

10. What do music lovers enjoy?

_ _ _ _ _ _ _ _ _ _

Break the Code Look at the code box. Each letter of a Core Word is represented by another letter. Use the code to write Core Words.

Letter	a	b	c	d	e	f	g	h	i	j	k	l	m	n	o	p	q	r	s	t	u	v	w	x	y	z
Code	p	q	r	s	t	u	v	w	x	y	z	a	b	c	d	e	f	g	h	i	j	k	l	m	n	o

11. **trwd**   12. **otgdh**   13. **edipid**   14. **wtgdth**   15. **idbpid**

Use the Dictionary A dictionary entry sometimes includes a sentence in which the entry word is used. The sentence shows the meaning of the entry word. Look up these words in your Speller Dictionary. Use each word below in a sentence of your own that shows the word's meaning.

16. echo   17. hero   18. zero

WRITE ON YOUR OWN

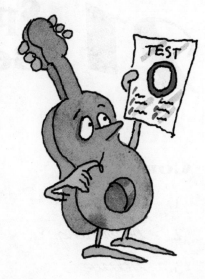

Write an announcement for a special concert. Tell where and when it will take place and add some details to attract an audience. Use at least four Core Words from this lesson.

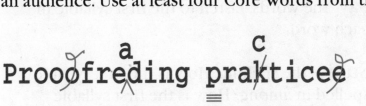

Prooofreding prakticee
a   c

1–4. Here is a draft of one student's announcement. Find four misspelled Core Words and write them correctly.

At 2:00 p.m. on sunday, June 5 1994, the music of the rock group Hot Potatoes will echoe through the trees of scalzi Park in Portland Maine. Portland's local heros Leo and James Lewis will be playing electric pianoes. The concert is free and will also be broadcast on radeo station WDVT.

5–8. This student forgot to capitalize two proper nouns and left out two commas—one between a day and year and the other between a city and state. Copy the announcement and correct the errors.

Now proofread your own announcement and correct any errors.

CORE			CHALLENGE
potato	tomatoes	radio	studios
potatoes	piano	radios	centuries
zero	pianos	echo	rodeos
zeros	hero	echoes	glossaries
tomato	heroes	mosquitoes	dynamos

21 Spelling Words Beginning with *a* or *be*

CORE

1. among
2. beginning
3. believe
4. award
5. betray
6. between
7. arise
8. behave
9. behind
10. amuse
11. belong
12. beyond
13. agree
14. become
15. asleep

Say the words. Listen to the first syllable in each word.

Study the spelling. How is the first syllable spelled in *among?* How is the first syllable spelled in *beginning?*

Write the words.

1–6. Write the Core Words that begin with the syllable *a.*

7–15. Write the Core Words that begin with the syllable *be.*

16–20. Write the Challenge Words. Circle the word that begins with the syllable *a.* Underline the words that begin with the syllable *be.*

SPELLING TIP
Many words begin with the syllable *a* or *be.*

CHALLENGE

16. beneath
17. bewilder
18. above
19. bewitch
20. bestow

WORDS and MEANINGS

Write the Core Words that best complete the story.

About Columbus

As a boy Christopher Columbus liked to (1) himself by watching ships. His days were filled with thoughts of ships. At night, after he fell (2), he dreamed of sailing the seas and discovering what lay (3) his own part of the world.

Years later, when Columbus had (4) a sailor, he had an unusual idea. He wanted to sail west to reach China. Most people did not (5) this could be done. However, Columbus persuaded the king and queen of Spain to (6) to pay for his trip. They were (7) the few people who supported his idea.

During the journey (8) Spain and America, problems began to (9). The crew started to (10) badly. They plotted (11) Columbus's back to (12) him. Luckily for Columbus their plan fell through.

On October 12, 1492, the crew sighted land. They decided that the land should (13) to Spain. Columbus received great honors and an (14). His discovery of the New World was the (15) of a remarkable period in history.

The Suffix -ment

The suffix -ment can mean "the state of being ___." For example, amusement means "the state of being amused." Write a definition of each word below. Begin each definition with "the state of being."

16. agreement
17. disappointment
18. excitement
19. contentment
20. amazement
21. puzzlement
22. employment

Word Play

Locate the Ships Each capital letter and number is the location of a ship on the chart. For example, *D4* (row D, column 4) is the location of ship *y*. Find all the ships in each group. Use the letters on the ships to write a Core Word.

1. E1 B2 D4 E4 D2 C5
2. C3 A1 E4 D2 A4
3. E1 B2 C1 B5 C3 D4
4. C3 A4 B5 B2 B2
5. E1 B2 E3 E4 A1 B2
6. E1 B2 A2 E4 D2 A4

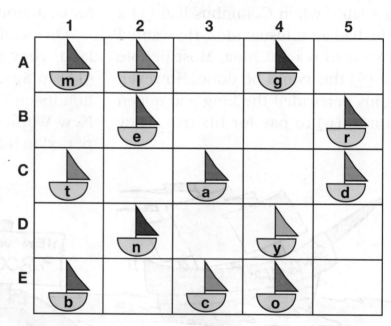

Look, Listen, and Write Write one or two Core Words that fit each clue.

7. This word has the /ôr/ sound spelled *ar*.
8–9. These words have the long *i* sound.
10. In this word, a letter was doubled when an ending was added.
11. This word has the /ū/ sound spelled *u-e*.
12. In this word the long *e* sound is not spelled *ea* or *ee*.

Think and Write Write the Core Word that completes each statement.

13. *Top* is to *middle* as *above* is to ___.
14. *Talk* is to *speak* as *act* is to ___.
15. *Begin* is to *end* as *awake* is to ___.

Write a journal entry that a sailor on Columbus's ship might have written on October 12, 1492. Use at least four Core Words from this lesson.

Prooofreding prakticee

1–5. Here is a draft of one student's journal entry. Find five misspelled Core Words and write them correctly.

> October 12, 1492— Just as I was baginning to think this journey would never end, we spotted a thin strip of land biyond the blue water. I could hardly believe my eyes! With so many miles of ocean buhind us, only a few more miles lay batween our ship and land. I pinched myself to make sure I was not esleep.

Now proofread your own journal entry and correct any errors.

CORE			CHALLENGE
among	between	belong	beneath
beginning	arise	beyond	bewilder
believe	behave	agree	above
award	behind	become	bewitch
betray	amuse	asleep	bestow

Spelling Singular and Plural Possessive Nouns

CORE

1. babies'
2. referee's
3. officer's
4. ladies'
5. director's
6. actress's
7. parents'
8. waiter's
9. owner's
10. buyers'
11. pilot's
12. actor's
13. students'
14. lady's
15. baby's

CHALLENGE

16. athletes'
17. octopus's
18. astronauts'
19. triceratops's
20. operators'

Say the words. Listen for the final /s/ and /z/ sounds.

Study the spelling. Which word means "belonging to one lady"? Which word means "belonging to more than one lady"? How is *baby* changed to a possessive noun? How is *babies* changed to a possessive noun?

Write the words.

1–10. Write the Core Words that are singular and possessive.

11–15. Write the Core Words that are plural and possessive.

16–20. Write the Challenge Words. Circle the words that are singular and possessive. Underline the words that are plural and possessive.

SPELLING TIP

The possessive of a singular noun is usually formed by adding an apostrophe and *s*.
The possessive of a plural noun that ends in *s* is usually formed by adding only an apostrophe.

WORDS and MEANINGS

Write the Core Words that best complete the story.

The Students' Big Sale

Last week our class held a big sidewalk sale outside the school. The sale was very well organized. One student was chosen to direct the sale, and the other students followed the (1) orders. Several of the (2) parents also helped out. The (3) job was to help us price the items.

People had donated some great stuff to sell. There was a photo of an actress with the (4) autograph. There was a video starring a famous actor, showing the best performance of the (5) career. There was a police (6) badge and a basketball (7) whistle. There was a (8) tray and an airplane (9) helmet. There was a (10) crib and enough toys to fill a dozen (11) playpens. Also, several ladies had donated jewelry. Those (12) jewelry and another (13) silk shawl were items that sold quickly.

Everything went pretty smoothly. Someone lost a wallet, but it contained the (14) name and was soon returned. The sale itself was a big success. It was fun to see the delighted grins on the (15) faces when they walked away with their treasures.

Possessives of Unusual Plurals

Some plural words do not end in *s*. The possessive of these plurals is formed by adding an apostrophe and *s*. Change each word below to a plural possessive.

16. goose
17. woman
18. mouse

19. tooth
20. man

Complete the Titles

Write the Core Word that best completes each book title. Begin each word with a capital letter.

1. The _____ Guide to Raising Children by U. B. Goode

2. CHOOSING YOUR _____ NAME by Howie Callem

3. A _____ POLICE LIFE by I. C. CROOKS

4. The CAR _____ REPAIR MANUAL by Hope E. Startz

5. Getting Your Airplane _____ License by Izzy Reddy

6. Smart GUIDE TO EVEN BETTER GRADES By Rita Lott

Get to the Core

Write Core Words to answer the questions.

7. Which word spells the long *a* sound with *ai*?

8. Which word contains a homophone of *by*?

9–10. In which two words was the final *y* changed when an ending was added?

11–12. Which two words contain a long *e* sound that is not spelled *ee* or *ie*?

13–14. Which two words form a male and female pair?

15. Which word's base word is *refer*?

16. Which three-syllable word is stressed on the second syllable?

Write an article for a school newspaper about a special event that took place at the school. Follow the writing process steps on pages 134–135 to write your article. Use at least four Core Words from this lesson.

Proofreding prakticee

1–5. Here is a draft of one student's article. Find five misspelled Core Words and write them correctly.

> This year's relay races were a great success. The ticket buyers's line stretched across the whole playground. When the referee' whistle sounded and the first race began, little could be heard above the parent's cheers. In one race, each student had to carry a full glass of water on a waiters's tray. Most students trays ended up pretty wet.

Now proofread your own article and correct any errors.

CORE			CHALLENGE
babies'	actress's	pilot's	athletes'
referee's	parents'	actor's	octopus's
officer's	waiter's	students'	astronauts'
ladies'	owner's	lady's	triceratops's
director's	buyers'	baby's	operators'

23 Spelling the Names of Body Parts

FOCUS

CORE

1. lungs
2. tendons
3. ligament
4. skull
5. plasma
6. appendix
7. spinal cord
8. marrow
9. nerves
10. vein
11. kidney
12. skeleton
13. artery
14. stomach
15. tonsils

CHALLENGE

16. muscles
17. esophagus
18. vertebrae
19. bloodstream
20. epidermis

Say each word. Listen for familiar vowel and consonant sounds.

Study the spelling. Can you find familiar vowel spellings? What other familiar spellings do you find?

Write the words.

- **1–4.** Write the Core Words that have one syllable.

- **5–10.** Write the Core Words that have two syllables.

- **11–15.** Write the Core Words that have three syllables.

- **16–20.** Write the Challenge Words. Circle any consonant blends you find. Draw a line between the two words that make up a compound word.

SPELLING TIP
Many names of body parts follow expected spellings. Others have spellings that must be remembered.

Words and Meanings

Write the Core Words that best complete the story.

Head to Toe

Imagine that you could travel through the human body. Start inside the bony framework of the head, called the (1). There you see bundles of (2) that carry messages from the brain. As you move downward into the mouth, you see two (3) at the back of the throat. Approaching the heart, you come to the main (4) that carries blood away from the heart. A little below that is the main (5) that brings blood back to the heart. Blood is composed of red blood cells and a yellow liquid called (6).

Your next stop is a pair of organs for breathing, called (7). Nearby, food passes down your throat to the (8), where digestion begins. Behind the stomach is a pair of organs. Each of these, a (9), filters liquid waste from the blood and passes it to the bladder. The long tubes called intestines also help with digestion. Attached to the large intestine is a small organ called the (10), which may be removed if it becomes inflamed.

The bones in the human body make up the (11). Inside most bones is (12), which produces blood cells. Inside the backbone is nerve tissue that makes up the (13). One bone is connected to another by a kind of tissue called a (14). Other bands of tissue, called (15), attach bones to muscles.

The Suffix -*itis*

The suffix -*itis* means "inflammation of." Complete each definition below with a Core Word.

16. *Tonsillitis* means "inflammation of the ___."

17. *Tendonitis* means "inflammation of the ___."

18. *Appendicitis* means "inflammation of the ___."

Lesson 23   85

Complete the Diagram
Write the Core Words that are missing from the diagram.

1-4.

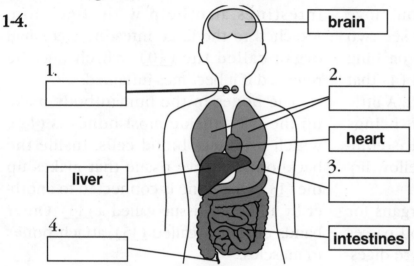

brain

1. _____

2. _____

heart

3. _____

liver

4. _____

intestines

Look, Listen, and Write
Write one or more Core Words that answer each question.

5-9. Which words begin with a consonant blend?

10-12. Which words have double consonants?

13. Which word is a homophone for *vane* and *vain?*

14. Which one-syllable word has the /ûr/ sound that you hear in *worse?*

Match the Endings
Write the Core Word that has the same last syllable as each word below.

15. government   16. pardons   17. battery   18. chimney

Use the Dictionary
Look up these words in your Speller Dictionary. Write each word given below and draw a line between the syllables, like this: *mar/row.* Then underline each stressed syllable.

19. skeleton   20. ligament   21. stomach   22. appendix

Write a brochure for National Health Week. List things people do to protect their health. Use at least four Core Words.

Prooofreding prakticee

(proofreading corrections: delete *o* in "Prooofreding", insert *a*; insert *c* in "prakticee", delete final *e*)

1–4. Here is a draft of one student's list. Find four misspelled Core Words and write them correctly.

> Quit smoking. Give your lungs a chance to breathe.
> Say no to tea and coffee. They are bad for your nirves.
> Cut down on fatty foods. They can cause a blocked arterry.
> Stand up straight Good posture is good for your spinel cord.
> Do you ride a bike. Wear a helmet to protect your scull.

5–6. This student left out one period and used one incorrect end punctuation mark. Copy the list and correct the errors.

Now proofread your own list and correct any errors.

CORE			CHALLENGE
lungs	appendix	kidney	muscles
tendons	spinal cord	skeleton	esophagus
ligament	marrow	artery	vertebrae
skull	nerves	stomach	bloodstream
plasma	vein	tonsils	epidermis

Combine the words and endings to make a Core Word from Lesson 19.

1. plan + *ed*
2. garden + *ing*
3. drop + *ed*
4. trace + *ing*

Write the Core Word from Lesson 20 that is the plural of each word below.

5. tomato
6. zero
7. hero
8. piano

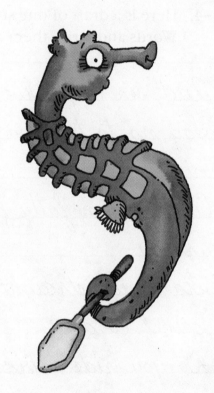

Write a Core Word from Lesson 21 that means the opposite of the underlined word or phrase in each sentence.

9. Does Uncle Frank always <u>bore</u> you with his stories?
10. Did the children act <u>naughty</u> at the wedding?
11. They <u>doubt</u> that Suzie comes from Canada.
12. Dad was <u>awake</u> when the phone rang.

REVIEW

Write a Core Word from Lesson 22 to complete each tongue twister. The missing word will be the possessive of the underlined word.

13. The play bees of the <u>babies</u> are the ___ play bees!

14. The driers of the <u>buyers</u> are the ___ driers!

15. The tractor of the <u>actor</u> is an ___ tractor.

16. A detector belonging to a <u>director</u> is a ___ detector.

Write each phrase or sentence below. Replace the underlined word or words with a Core Word from Lesson 23. Each missing word will be a part of the body. The corrected phrase or sentence is a famous quotation.

17. "A custom loathsome to the eye, hateful to the nose, harmful to the brain, dangerous to the <u>organs one breathes with</u>."

    — *JAMES I OF ENGLAND* (speaking of tobacco)

18. "I am cruelly used, nobody feels for my poor <u>fibers that carry messages to the brain</u>."

    — *JANE AUSTEN*

19. "Down to the Puritan <u>soft tissue</u> of my bones there's something in this richness that I hate." — *ELINOR HOYT WYLIE*

20. "An army marches on its <u>organ that digests food</u>."

    — *NAPOLEON*

25 Spelling Words with the Prefix *dis-* or *mis-*

CORE

1. disconnect
2. misjudge
3. disappear
4. mislaid
5. disagree
6. mislead
7. discover
8. misprint
9. disloyal
10. mismatch
11. displease
12. misspell
13. disgrace
14. mistreat
15. distrust

CHALLENGE

16. misfortune
17. disappoint
18. mispronounce
19. dishonest
20. misunderstand

Prefix	+ Word	= New Word
dis-	connect	= disconnect
mis-	judge	= misjudge

Say the words. Listen for the prefix and the base word.

Study the spelling. How is the prefix spelled in *disagree?* How is the prefix spelled in *misspell?* How does the prefix change the meaning of the base word?

Write the words.

    1–8. Write the Core Words that begin with the prefix **dis-**.

    9–15. Write the Core Words that begin with the prefix **mis-**.

  16–20. Write the Challenge Words. Circle the prefix in each word.

SPELLING TIP

Many words begin with the prefix **dis-,** which means "not" or "opposite."
Many words begin with the prefix **mis-,** which means "badly" or "wrongly."

A Rabbit's Misbehavior

I work hard at being a good magician and hope never to (1) my audience. But one day everything went wrong. First, there was a (2) on the invitation to my show. The printer had managed to (3) the name of the street. He got the phone number right, though, and the phone rang so much that I wanted to (4) it. Then I (5) my magic hat and almost had to start without it.

But the real problem was my rabbit, Clyde. My best trick is putting Clyde into my hat and making him (6). But that day Clyde simply refused to vanish. Imagine how foolish I felt! Clyde had caused me to (7) myself.

After the show I spoke sternly to Clyde. "How could you be so (8) to me? Did I ever hurt you or (9) you? Why did you (10) me into believing that you would vanish? It is a sad thing to (11) that a rabbit whom you once trusted now fills you with (12). I used to think we were the perfect partners. Now, though, I think we are a complete (13)!"

Clyde replied, "I (14) with you. We are fine partners. And if you think I am such a bad rabbit, then you (15) me. I am a very good rabbit, but sometimes I just get tired of this vanishing act."

More Words with *mis-* or *dis-*
Write a word to match each phrase that begins with *mis-* or *dis-*.

mis-	*dis-*
16. behave badly	20. not approve
17. state incorrectly	21. opposite of *comfort*
18. read incorrectly	22. not believe
19. use wrongly	

Discover the Words

1–8. The base words of eight Core Words are hidden in the magician's scarf. Add prefixes to them and write the Core Words.

splkdifjlprint
akdjtktrustie
orldagreeks
thecovernvllw
aleadtkdown
xloyalkodxheb
wottreatkso
iothlaidksn

Look, Listen, and Write Write one or more Core Words that fit each clue.

   9. It has the /j/ sound spelled in two different ways.
10–12. They have double consonants.
   13. It has the /s/ sound spelled *ce*.
   14. It has the same base word as *pleasant*.
   15. It has the letter *t*, but no /t/ sound.

Use the Dictionary Look up the underlined prefix of each word below in your Speller Dictionary. Then write a definition for the word.

16. <u>mis</u>file 17. <u>pre</u>view 18. <u>re</u>place 19. <u>un</u>even 20. <u>non</u>sense

Write a review of a magic show or any live show that you have seen or would like to see. Describe some of the tricks and tell what you liked or did not like about the show. Follow the writing process steps on pages 134–135 to write your review. Use at least four Core Words from this lesson.

Prooofreding prakticee
a   c

1–5. Here is a draft of one student's review. Find five misspelled Core Words and write them correctly.

> Few will dissagree that Wanda Maze gave a fine show. She pretended to have myslaid her magic wand, and then pulled it out of her ear. She made a cat dissappear. She gave a boy two linked metal rings and told him to diconnect them. When he could not, she quickly pulled them apart. The boy checked the rings but could not descover how the trick worked.

Now proofread your own review and correct any errors.

CORE			CHALLENGE
disconnect	mislead	displease	misfortune
misjudge	discover	misspell	disappoint
disappear	misprint	disgrace	mispronounce
mislaid	disloyal	mistreat	dishonest
disagree	mismatch	distrust	misunderstand

26 Spelling Unstressed Vowels

CORE

1. falcon
2. stadium
3. captain
4. ballad
5. suppose
6. hasten
7. mountain
8. apron
9. period
10. villain
11. ballot
12. canyon
13. organ
14. parrot
15. carton

CHALLENGE

16. oxygen
17. pigeon
18. pollute
19. medicine
20. pelican

FOCUS

Sound	Spelling		
/ə/	hasten	apron	organ
	captain	suppose	

Say the words. Listen for the /ə/ sound, called the schwa, in unstressed syllables.

Study the spelling. How is the /ə/ sound spelled in each word?

Write the words.

1–12. Write the Core Words that have the /ə/ sound spelled with one letter. Circle the letters that spell the /ə/ sound.

13–15. Write the Core Words that have the /ə/ sound spelled with two letters. Circle the letters that spell the /ə/ sound.

16–20. Write the Challenge Words. Circle the letters that spell the /ə/ sound.

SPELLING TIP

The schwa sound occurs in the unstressed syllables of many words. It can be spelled *e, o, a, ai,* or *u.*

A Surprise Prize

The tickets for my favorite game show had come, and the big day was here. The studio audience was expected to be in costume, so I put on a cook's outfit with a white hat and an (1). Then I had to (2) to the studio.

The studio seats were arranged as they are in a (3). One man was dressed as the (4) of a ship. A woman near me was dressed as a (5) climber. Someone else was an evil (6), wearing a cape and mustache. A girl was dressed like a famous singer and even sang a (7).

I could hardly believe it when the host chose me to come onto the stage! He handed me $500 and asked whether I wanted to keep the money or take what was in the large (8) behind him. The box had a slot in the top, like a (9) box that voters use. As I was making up my mind, (10) music played in the background. I was given only a brief (11) in which to decide. "I (12) I'll take the box," I finally mumbled.

When I opened the box, a colorful (13) hopped out, calling "Surprise! Surprise!" I was thrilled, but glad that I wouldn't be taking home an eagle or a (14). A bird of prey would be much happier building a home in the walls of a (15).

The Suffix -ist

The suffix -ist adds the meaning "one who ___" to a base word. If a base word ends with a vowel, drop the vowel before adding -ist. Add -ist to each word and write the new word.

16. organ

17. type

18. cycle

19. piano

20. tour

Hidden Words
Write the Core Words that contain the smaller words below.

1. rot
2. lot
3. lad
4. ton

Guess My Roots
Write the Core Words that are most likely to come from the words and meanings below.

5. from Latin *mappa* meaning "napkin"
6. from Latin *caput* meaning "head"

Complete the Group
Write the Core Word that belongs in each group.

7. piano, harp, ___
8. comma, colon, ___
9. valley, crater, ___
10. think, believe, ___
11. crook, rascal, ___
12. hawk, eagle, ___

Look, Listen, and Write
Write Core Words to answer the questions.

13. Which word has a silent *t*?
14. Which word has the vowel sound you hear in *cow*?
15–16. Which words have the long *e* sound spelled *i*?

WRITE ON YOUR OWN

Imagine that you are an announcer on a game show. Your job is to tell the audience what the prizes will be. Write your announcement. Use at least four Core Words from this lesson.

Prooofreding prakticee

1-4. Here is a draft of one student's announcement. Find four misspelled Core Words and write them correctly.

> Today's winner will visit the Grand Canyan for a periud of one week, all expenses paid The runner-up will go to a basketball game at grover Stadium and have dinner with the captian of the team. the rest of the contestants will each receive a carten containing 50 cans of Yum-Yum Dog Food

5-8. This student forgot to capitalize a proper noun and the first word of a sentence and left out two periods. Copy the announcement and correct the errors.

Now proofread your own announcement and correct any errors.

CORE			CHALLENGE
falcon	hasten	ballot	oxygen
stadium	mountain	canyon	pigeon
captain	apron	organ	pollute
ballad	period	parrot	medicine
suppose	villain	carton	pelican

27 Spelling Words with -*ent* and -*ant*

FOCUS

CORE

1. recent
2. absent
3. confident
4. represent
5. different
6. important
7. apparent
8. accident
9. tolerant
10. evident
11. resident
12. prominent
13. assistant
14. dependent
15. permanent

Say the words. Listen for the last syllable of each word. Does the last syllable sound the same in each word?

Study the spelling. How is the vowel sound spelled in the last syllable of *different?* How is the vowel sound spelled in the last syllable of *assistant?*

Write the words.

1–12. Write the Core Words that end with -*ent*.

13–15. Write the Core Words that end with -*ant*.

16–20. Write the Challenge Words. Circle the letter that spells the vowel sound in the last syllable of each word.

SPELLING TIP
Many words end with -*ent* or -*ant*. Their spellings must be remembered.

CHALLENGE

16. efficient
17. immigrant
18. indignant
19. transparent
20. significant

WORDS and MEANINGS

Write the Core Words that best complete the story.

A Campaign Event

At a town meeting held in the (1) past, Mary Amato, a candidate for mayor, was (2) due to an illness. However, she sent her (3), Sam Hampton, to (4) her. Although Hampton has not lived in Meadow Brook for long, his friendly smile and (5) chin have become familiar to all. When he got up to speak, it was (6) that he was not well prepared, because he had to read from his notes. Nevertheless, he gave a good speech.

"Ladies and gentlemen," he said, "if Mary Amato is elected mayor, all who visit Meadow Brook will want to make this town their (7) home. Every (8) of Meadow Brook will feel (9) that the streets are safe. There will be enough jobs to assure that no one will be (10) on charity. But these changes will not happen by (11). They will take hard work and cooperation. We must all learn how (12) it is to get along with one another. We must learn

to be (13) of people who come from (14) backgrounds."

It was (15) from the audience that many people agreed.

The Endings -*ence* and -*ance*

Many words that end in -*ent* or -*ant* are adjectives. By changing the ending to -*ence* or -*ance*, you can make these words nouns. Change these adjectives to nouns.

16. confident
17. different
18. important

19. tolerant
20. evident
21. prominent

22. dependent
23. permanent
24. absent

Praise the Candidate At this rally, some of the candidate's supporters have their signs turned the wrong way. Figure out the missing letters and write the Core Words that describe the candidate.

Terry for President

1. _ O _ / _ I D / _ N T
2. _ _ / _ E R / _ N T
3. _ _ P / _ R _ / _ N T
4. D / _ _ / _ E _ / _ N T

Think and Write. If a word is blue, write a Core Word that is a synonym for the word. If the word is red, write a Core Word that is an antonym for it.

5. dweller   7. chance   9. lasting   11. ancient
6. present   8. aide   10. self-supporting

Take a Close Look Write the Core Word that matches each clue.

12. It has one *o* and two *n*'s but no *d*.
13. It has a double consonant but no *i*.
14. It has two *e*'s and one *i* but no *r*.
15. It has one *p*, one *n*, and three *e*'s.

Use the Dictionary Write each word and then look up its pronunciation in your Speller Dictionary. Circle any letter that spells the /ə/ sound.

16. permanent   17. apparent   18. accident   19. dependent   20. prominent

Write a speech that could be given by someone running for a school or community office. Follow the writing process steps on pages 134–135 to write your speech. Use at least four Core Words from this lesson.

Prooofreding prakticee

1–5. Here is a draft of one student's speech. Find five misspelled Core Words and write them correctly.

> I am confidant that I am your best choice for president of the fifth-grade class. My leadership skills are evidint. I helped to plan the recint talent show, and I was an assistent on Parents' Night. My attendance record is also notable. I have been absunt from school only twice since first grade. Please let me be the one to represent you.

Now proofread your own speech and correct any errors.

CORE			CHALLENGE
recent	important	resident	efficient
absent	apparent	prominent	immigrant
confident	accident	assistant	indignant
represent	tolerant	dependent	transparent
different	evident	permanent	significant

28 Spelling Compound Words

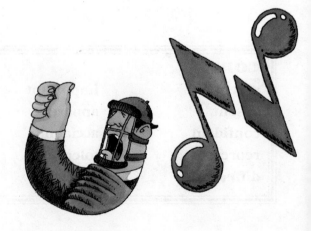

CORE

1. raincoat
2. handshake
3. motorcycle
4. roadblock
5. bedspread
6. birthplace
7. arrowhead
8. halfback
9. earthquake
10. newspaper
11. floodlight
12. underbrush
13. sweatshirt
14. drawbridge
15. sunglasses

Say the words. Listen for the two smaller words you hear in each word.

Study the spelling. What are the two smaller words you find in each word?

Write the words.

1–15. Write the Core Words. Draw a line between the two smaller words that make up each word.

16–20. Write the Challenge Words. Draw a line between the two smaller words that make up each word.

SPELLING TIP
Many words are made up of two smaller words. Words made up of smaller words are called compound words.

CHALLENGE

16. troublemaker
17. snapshot
18. bodyguard
19. needlepoint
20. straightforward

Good Times with an Old Friend

My friend Ashley greeted me at the train with a big smile and a warm (1). Before I moved away, Ashley and I had been best friends. For a long time now I had been looking forward to seeing her again and to revisiting my (2).

It took a while to reach Ashley's house. We sat in traffic while a (3) opened to let some boats pass. Then a police officer on a (4) stopped our car. He warned Ashley's dad of a (5) ahead, so we had to take a detour.

When we got to Ashley's house, we had a picnic in the yard. It was already dark, but the yard was lit up by a (6). We sat on the ground, using an old striped (7) as a blanket.

The next day we left to go camping. Since showers were likely, I had a (8). For cold nights, I had a puffy jacket that made me look like a football (9). For in-between weather, I had a cozy (10). For sunny days, I had a pair of (11).

Two exciting things happened on that trip. One day I found an Indian (12) in the (13) that grew near our campsite. Another day we felt the ground shake and realized it was a small (14). Until then, I had only read about such things in the (15)!

More Compound Words

Combine two words from the box to form a compound word that fits each definition.

horn	card	brush	snow	yard
storm	fog	back	board	tooth

16. thick paper used for boxes
17. land behind a home
18. an object for cleaning teeth
19. a horn warning boats in the fog
20. a blizzard

Write on Target
Each arrow has a number and a word on it. If the number is 1, write the first letter of the word. If the number is 2, write the second letter, and so on. When unscrambled, the letters will spell part of a Core Word. Write the complete Core Words.

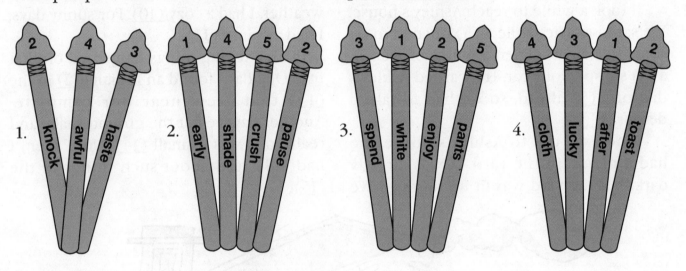

1. [2 knock] [4 awful] [3 haste]
2. [1 early] [4 shade] [5 crush] [2 pause]
3. [3 spend] [1 white] [2 enjoy] [5 pants]
4. [4 cloth] [3 lucky] [1 after] [2 toast]

Look, Listen, and Write
Write Core Words to answer the questions.

5. Which word has the long *i* sound spelled *igh*?
6. Which word has two short *a* sounds?
7. Which word has the /ô/ sound?
8. Which word has the /ûr/ sound and a short *e* sound?
9–10. Which two words have the /ûr/ sound and a long *a* sound?
11. Which word ends with the /əl/ sound?
12. Which word has the short *e* sound spelled two different ways?

Jump Back and Spell
Replace each letter below with the letter of the alphabet that comes before it. For example, replace *b* with *a*, *c* with *b*, and so on. Write the Core Words you find.

13. voefscsvti   14. iboetiblf   15. spbecmpdl

Imagine that you are on a trip visiting a friend. Write a letter home about something unusual that has happened. Follow the writing process steps on pages 134–135 to write your letter. Use at least four Core Words from this lesson.

Proo͏ofreding prakticeͤ

1–4. Here is a draft of one student's letter. Find four misspelled Core Words and write them correctly.

Dear Mom,

Guess what! There was an earth quake here. Did you read about it in the news-paper. A drawbrige was damaged, and a man fell off a motorcycle. No one was hurt on Mark's street, but Mrs Chang's sun glasses fell off a counter and broke.

5–6. This student used one incorrect end punctuation mark and left out a period after an abbreviation. Copy the letter and correct the errors.

Now proofread your own letter and correct any errors.

CORE			CHALLENGE
raincoat	birthplace	floodlight	troublemaker
handshake	arrowhead	underbrush	snapshot
motorcycle	halfback	sweatshirt	bodyguard
roadblock	earthquake	drawbridge	needlepoint
bedspread	newspaper	sunglasses	straightforward

Spelling Discoveries and Inventions

FOCUS

CORE

1. gravity
2. laser
3. sonar
4. electricity
5. camera
6. combine
7. telephone
8. automobile
9. transistor
10. microchip
11. airplane
12. television
13. skyscraper
14. microscope
15. radar

CHALLENGE

16. antibiotics
17. submarine
18. helicopter
19. refrigeration
20. stethoscope

Say the words. Listen for familiar vowel and consonant sounds.

Study the spelling. Can you find familiar long and short vowel spellings? What other familiar spellings do you find?

Write the words.

1-5. Write the Core Words that have two syllables.

6-12. Write the Core Words that have three syllables.

13-14. Write the Core Words that have four syllables.

15. Write the Core Word that has five syllables.

16-20. Write the Challenge Words. Underline the words with five syllables.

SPELLING TIP
Many words for important discoveries and inventions have familiar spellings.

WORDS and MEANINGS

Write the Core Words that best complete the story.

A Step Ahead

Human feats have ranged from the building of the tallest (1) to the discovery of the tiny atom. Back in the 1600s, farming was advanced by the invention of the (2), which was used to thresh grain. Later inventions changed the way people communicate. The (3) made it possible for people to record events through photographs. The (4) allowed people to talk to each other over great distances.

Edison's work with (5) produced the lightbulb. Then, in the middle of this century, the (6) was invented. It led to the creation of smaller radios and (7) sets. Later came two inventions for locating objects. One was (8), which uses radio waves to locate objects in space. The other was (9), which uses sound waves to locate objects under water.

Henry Ford's ideas for the (10) began a new era in transportation. With the birth of the (11), humans were able to overcome (12) and fly.

Medicine, too, has benefited from inventions. The (13) is used to study bacteria. Recently, doctors have been able to use a (14) to remove diseased body tissue. The computer (15) also aids in the treatment of disease.

The Prefix *micro-*

The prefix **micro-** means "very small." *Microscope,* for example, means "a scope for very small objects." Use **micro-** to write a word that fits each meaning.

16. very small film
17. a very small wave
18. a very small part of a second

Input the Inventions The computer screen shows a menu of
discoveries and inventions. They are listed in alphabetical order.
Write the Core Words that go in the blanks.

IMPORTANT INVENTIONS AND DISCOVERIES

atom
1. _____
bacteria
Braille
cash register
2. _____
compass
computer
3. _____
gasoline
irrigation

4. _____
lightbulb
loom
magnetism
5. _____
6. _____
moving pictures
nuclear power
printing press
7. _____
satellite

sewing machine
8. _____
9. _____
steam engine
tape recorder
10. _____
telescope
vitamins
x rays

Subtract and Spell Subtract the word shown from each group of letters.
Write the Core Word that remains.

11. vteildeevoitasipone - videotape
12. mgargnaevtisitym - magnetism
13. apriroppelllaenre - propeller

14. mtircaronswisatover - microwave
15. cnaegmateirvae - negative

Use the Dictionary Look up each underlined Core Word in your
Speller Dictionary. Write the definition that shows how the word is used
in the sentence.

16. The combine made the farmer's work easier.
17. Dancing is a way to combine exercise and fun.
18. She threw the ball high, but gravity brought it back.
19. By nightfall the lost hikers understood the gravity of their problem.
20. I will telephone you if I hear any news.

Choose an invention that you use a lot. Then write an essay about why this invention is so important. Follow the writing process steps on pages 134–135 to write your essay. Use at least four Core Words from this lesson.

Prooofreding prakticee

1–5. Here is a draft of one student's essay. Find five misspelled Core Words and write them correctly.

For me, the most important invention is the air plane. Without it, I could not see my favorite relatives. The telophone and camra are also important. They let me talk to my relatives and see their faces between visits. I write letters on a computer, so the micrachip is important. And none of these inventions would work without electrisity.

Now proofread your own essay and correct any errors.

CORE			CHALLENGE
gravity	combine	airplane	antibiotics
laser	telephone	television	submarine
sonar	automobile	skyscraper	helicopter
electricity	transistor	microscope	refrigeration
camera	microchip	radar	stethoscope

Write a Core Word from Lesson 25 that means the same as each underlined word below. Each word will begin with **dis-** or **mis-**.

1. It's a <u>shame</u> to toss litter on the street.

2. June and I always <u>argue</u> about what video to rent.

3. The <u>lost</u> mitten reappeared when the snow melted.

4. Whenever I watch a mystery, I always <u>suspect</u> the wrong character!

Write each phrase or sentence below. Replace the underlined word or words with a Core Word from Lesson 26. Each word will have the unstressed /ə/ sound. The new phrase or sentence is a famous quotation.

5. "...so do our minutes <u>hurry</u> toward their end..."
   — *WILLIAM SHAKESPEARE*

6. "How will you cross the autumn <u>large hill</u> alone?"
   — *OKU* (Japanese princess and poet)

7. "...the grand old <u>song that tells a story</u> of Sir Patrick Spence..."
   — *SAMUEL TAYLOR COLERIDGE*

8. "...a <u>bird of prey</u>, towering in her pride of place..."
   — *WILLIAM SHAKESPEARE*

Write a Core Word from Lesson 27 that means the opposite of each word below. Each word will end with -**ant** or -**ent**.

9. same
10. present
11. unsure
12. long-ago

Write a Core Word from Lesson 28 that fits each group of words. Each word you write will be a compound word.

13. storm, umbrella, boots, ___
14. sheet, blanket, pillow, ___
15. castle, moat, defense, ___
16. magazine, articles, daily, ___

Write a Core Word from Lesson 29 to complete each sentence. Each word will describe a discovery or invention and begin with the same letter as the underlined word.

17. The kids <u>turned</u> on the ___ and watched cartoons.

18. An <u>engineer</u> switched off the ___.

19. The young surgeon is <u>learning</u> to use the ___ to perform operations.

20. A ___ can <u>catch</u> brief moments and make them last.

31 Spelling Words with Silent Letters

CORE

1. folk
2. debt
3. column
4. wrench
5. gnaw
6. aisle
7. wrinkle
8. autumn
9. doubt
10. rhyme
11. bristle
12. sword
13. gnarled
14. listen
15. wrestle

CHALLENGE

16. solemn
17. campaign
18. rhythm
19. condemn
20. foreign

Say the words. Listen for the vowel and consonant sounds.

Study the spelling. Look for letters that are not pronounced. Which letters are silent in *folk* and *debt?* Which letters are silent in *column* and *gnaw?*

Write the words.

1–15. Write the Core Words. Circle the silent letters.

16–17. Write the Challenge Words that have a silent *n*.

18–20. Write the Challenge Words that have a silent *g* or *h*. Circle the silent letters.

SPELLING TIP
Some words contain silent letters. Their spellings must be remembered.

WORDS and MEANINGS

Write the Core Words that best complete the story.

The Magic Cure

An old (1) legend tells of a queen who became very ill. The only thing that could cure her was a (2) from the back of an enchanted porcupine. One day in (3), a young maid arrived at the castle. Beside a tall (4) stood a guard with a long, gleaming (5). The maid walked past the guard and down the (6) to the queen's throne. "I've come to help," the maid said.

"I (7) that you can help me," the queen said sadly. She had a worried (8) between her brows, and her hands were twisted and (9). But the maid would not (10) to the queen. That very day she set off to the woods to find the porcupine. At last she

saw him. He had stopped to (11) on a branch. She sprang from behind a tree, but the porcupine was too quick for her. "If you try to (12) a bristle from my back," he said, "I will (13) with you until you cry for mercy. But I will gladly give you a bristle if you can complete this (14): *Time passes with every season, but no one yet has found the....*"

"Reason!" cried the maid. Then she plucked a bristle and ran with it to the queen, who was instantly cured.

"I owe you a great (15)," the queen said.

MAGIC BRISTLES
QUICK CURE
CURE FOR THE QUEEN

WORD WORKS

Words with a Prefix and a Suffix

Many words have both a prefix and a suffix or verb ending. Write each word below. Underline the prefix and the suffix or verb ending.

16. unwrinkled
17. indebted
18. encouraging
19. mismanagement
20. recycler
21. impossiblity
22. distasteful
23. insincerely
24. unheroic

Rhyme with the Porcupine Find the words that rhyme with Core Words.

1–7. Seven of the words on the porcupine's bristles rhyme with Core Words. Write the seven Core Words.

Look, Listen, and Write Write the Core Word that fits each clue.

8. It begins with two consonants. Both are pronounced.
9. It has a past-tense ending.
10. It has the short *o* sound and the schwa sound.
11–13. Three words that spell the /ô/ sound three different ways.

Complete the Analogy Write the Core Word that completes each statement.

14. *Eye* is to *watch* as *ear* is to ___.
15. *Pound* is to *hammer* as *twist* is to ___.
16. *Wash* is to *dirt* as *iron* is to ___.

114   Lesson 31

WRITE ON YOUR OWN

Write a folktale in which magical things happen. Follow the writing process steps on pages 134–135 to write your story. Use at least four Core Words from this lesson.

Prooofreding prakticee

1-5. Here is a draft of the story that one student wrote. Find five misspelled words and write them correctly.

One fine autumm day, a knight was walking in the woods when he stopped to lissen to a lark. There he saw a deer that was bound up with a rope and trying to naw itself free. Feeling sorry for the deer, the knight cut the rope with his sord. To his amazement, the deer spoke. "Since I am in your det, I will be your servant," it said. And with that, the deer turned into a beautiful horse.

Now proofread your own story and correct any errors.

CORE			CHALLENGE
folk	aisle	bristle	solemn
debt	wrinkle	sword	campaign
column	autumn	gnarled	rhythm
wrench	doubt	listen	condemn
gnaw	rhyme	wrestle	foreign

32 Spelling Words with *ph* or *gh*

CORE

1. orphan
2. geography
3. elephant
4. alphabet
5. laugh
6. paragraph
7. telegraph
8. nephew
9. tough
10. phantom
11. photograph
12. enough
13. dolphin
14. triumph
15. trough

CHALLENGE

16. asphalt
17. typhoon
18. pharmacy
19. rough
20. triumphant

FOCUS

Sound	Spelling	
/f/	orphan	laugh

Say the words. Listen for the /f/ sound in each word.

Study the spelling. How is the /f/ sound spelled in *orphan?* How is it spelled in *laugh?*

Write the words.

1–11. Write the Core Words with the /f/ sound spelled *ph*. Underline the word that has the /f/ sound twice.

12–15. Write the Core Words with the /f/ sound spelled *gh*.

16–20. Write the Challenge Words. Circle the letters that spell the /f/ sound in each word.

SPELLING TIP
The /f/ sound can be spelled *ph* or *gh*.

WORDS and MEANINGS

Write the Core Words that best complete the story.

A Day at the Circus

My young (1) Stevie is an (2). One day I decided to take him to the circus.

At the sideshow we saw animals such as a lion and a huge gray (3). Outside each cage was a sign with a (4) or two telling about the animal. We read that elephants are gentle, yet (5) enough to do heavy work. We read that some chimpanzees can recognize letters of the (6). We also learned facts about the (7) of the land that each animal came from.

Inside the main tent was a large pool in which a trained (8) performed. A lady tapped out commands in Morse code, which is used to send messages by (9). The dolphin understood each command and responded with a trick. Next, a magician gave an amazing show, then disappeared in a puff of smoke like a (10). Then a clown nervously walked across a tightrope. She reached the end with a big smile of (11) but then fell into a (12) of water. That really made us (13). Stevie had brought a camera and took a (14).

By the end of the day we had seen (15) and were ready to head home.

The Word Part *tele-*

The word part *tele-* means "over a distance." A *telegraph* is something that writes over a distance. Write the word that fits each clue.

telemarketer   teleprinter   telecast
telemeter   telephoto

16. It takes photos from a distance.
17. It broadcasts from a distance.
18. It measures distance.

19. A person who sells goods from a distance.
20. It prints from a distance.

Juggle for a Spell
The number of balls each clown is juggling tells you how many syllables are in a certain Core Word. The letters on the balls are letters in that word. Write the Core Word.

1. A G E

2. O U

3. H R A P

4. H G O

5. M R

6. N P H

Get the Hint
Write the Core Word that matches each hint.

7. He belongs to your sister or brother.
8. It helps you find names in the phone book.
9. It is a furless, gray mammal without a long nose.
10. A clown's job is to produce this.

Use the Dictionary
Write the Core Word or Core Words that you would find on a dictionary page with these guide words.

11–12. paper/phonograph   **13–15.** total/tumbler   **16.** Neptune/outfit

WRITE ON YOUR OWN

Write an interview that might take place between a reporter and a circus performer. Write the reporter's questions and the performer's answers. Follow the writing process steps on pages 134-135. Use at least four Core Words from this lesson.

Prooofreding prakticee

a   c

1-5. Here is part of the interview that one student wrote. Find five misspelled words and write them correctly.

REPORTER: Is it true that making people lauf can be tough.

CLOWN: Not for me! just my face is enouph to make them howl.

REPORTER: Describe your most populas act?

CLOWN: I am teaching an elefant the alghabet, but he keeps dipping his trunk in a trouph and spraying the blackboard.

6-8. The student who wrote this interview used two incorrect end punctuation marks and did not capitalize the first word of one sentence. Copy her interview and correct the errors.

Now proofread your own interview and correct any errors.

CORE			CHALLENGE
orphan	paragraph	photograph	asphalt
geography	telegraph	enough	typhoon
elephant	nephew	dolphin	pharmacy
alphabet	tough	triumph	rough
laugh	phantom	trough	triumphant

33 Spelling the *-tion, -sion,* or *-sure* Endings

CORE

1. edition
2. explosion
3. discussion
4. position
5. measure
6. collision
7. promotion
8. mission
9. version
10. pleasure
11. selection
12. tradition
13. treasure
14. examination
15. restriction

CHALLENGE

16. commotion
17. construction
18. estimation
19. limitation
20. observation

FOCUS

Sound	Spelling	
/shən/	edition	mission
/zhən/	version	
/zhər/	measure	

Say the words. Listen for the final /shən/, /zhən/, or /zhər/ sounds in each word.

Study the spellings. How are the /shən/, /zhən/, and /zhər/ sounds spelled in each word?

Write the words.

1–9. Write the Core Words that end with the /shən/ sound you hear in *edition*.

10–15. Write the Core Words that end with the /zhən/ or /zhər/ sounds you hear in *version* and *measure*.

16–20. Write the Challenge Words. Underline the letters that spell /shən/.

SPELLING TIP

A final /shən/ is often spelled *-tion* or *-sion*. A final /zhən/ is often spelled *-sion*. A final /zhər/ is often spelled *-sure.*

Look to Books

Write the Core Words that best complete the story.

There is no way to (1) the value of reading, but we know that books educate and bring great (2) to people. Many book lovers even join (3) groups so they can talk about the books they read. Although books are often made into movies, the book (4) is usually much better. And books are available to everyone at no cost. Public libraries are an American (5), and every library has a large (6) of books on every subject.

Reading can prepare you for an (7) at school, or, if you are writing a report, you can gather facts from a recent (8) of an encyclopedia. At your job, reading can help you get a (9) to a higher (10).

If you like mysteries, you can read about the search for a stolen (11) or a spy on a secret (12). If you like science fiction, you can read about a spacecraft trying to avoid a (13) with a meteor or a dangerous experiment that could end in an (14) that would destroy the earth. If you long to travel but cannot afford to do it, reading allows you to travel without (15) in your imagination.

The Suffix -ary

The suffix -ary means "of." *Missionary* means "of a mission." Write a word with the suffix -ary for each meaning.

16. of honor
17. of a legend
18. of a moment

19. of a custom
20. of vision

Solve the Puzzles
On a separate piece of paper, write the two Core Words that would fit in each crossword puzzle.

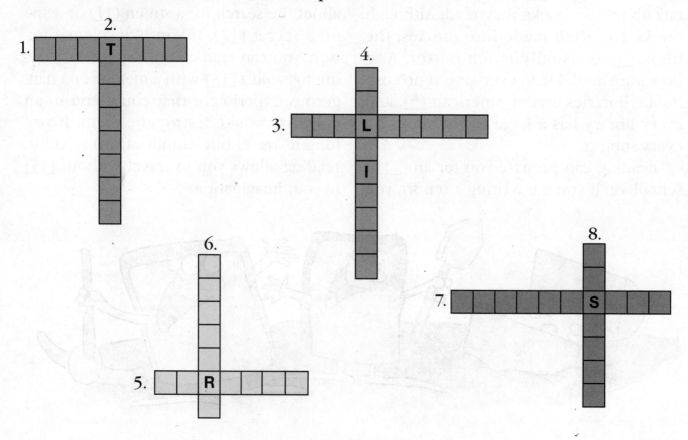

Dig for the Root
The underlined part of each word below comes from the same root as a Core Word. Write the Core Word.

9. <u>strict</u>ness   10. dis<u>please</u>   11. dis<u>miss</u>   12. de<u>posit</u>   13. e<u>motion</u>

Select the Synonym
Write the Core Word that is a synonym for each word below.

14. test   15. choice   16. custom   17. talk   18. crash

WRITE ON YOUR OWN

A book jacket often has a blurb—a brief advertisement or description—to tempt people to read the book. Write a blurb for the jacket of a book that you have enjoyed. Follow the writing process steps on pages 134–135. Use at least four Core Words from this lesson.

Proofreding prakticee

1–4. Here is a draft of the book-jacket blurb that one student wrote. Find four misspelled words and write them correctly.

> The Secret Garden is the story of a group of children with a special mishion. This new edision of the book, with its beautiful illustrations, is something to keep and treazure. It is a wonderful selecion for any child and will bring equal pleasure to adults.

Now proofread your own book-jacket blurb and correct any errors.

CORE			CHALLENGE
edition	collision	selection	commotion
explosion	promotion	tradition	construction
discussion	mission	treasure	estimation
position	version	examination	limitation
measure	pleasure	restriction	observation

34 Spelling the Names of Units of Measure

FOCUS

CORE

1. yards
2. millimeter
3. quart
4. acre
5. centimeter
6. teaspoon
7. ounces
8. gallon
9. liter
10. bushels
11. meter
12. minutes
13. volume
14. tablespoon
15. kilometer

CHALLENGE

16. leagues
17. eon
18. degree
19. decades
20. amperes

Say the words. Listen for familiar vowel and consonant sounds.

Study the spelling. Look for familiar and unusual spelling patterns. How is the long *e* sound spelled in *liter* and *meter?* How is the /ər/ sound spelled in *acre?* Which word parts do you see in several words?

Write the words.

1–11. Write the Core Words that have one or two syllables. Underline the words that have one syllable.

12–15. Write the Core Words that have three or four syllables. Circle the word that has three syllables.

16–20. Write the Challenge Words. Underline that word that has one syllable.

SPELLING TIP

Words that describe length, weight, or amount have many familiar spellings and word parts.

WORDS and MEANINGS

Write the Core Words that best complete the story.

A Day on the Farm

I live on a small farm. My family and I plow and plant every (1) of land ourselves. Today I made pancakes, but I had the wrong measuring spoon. It was a (2), which holds three times as much as a (3).

After breakfast I went to the barn, which is just a few (4) from the house. There I worked on the (5) of the rabbit cage to give the rabbits more space. The height was to be one (6), or a little more than three feet. I was using wood with a thickness of a (7), or a little less than half an inch. I tried to measure carefully so I would not be off by even a (8), which is only a tiny fraction of an inch. After I had been there only a few (9), my father came by to pick up some fuel we had stored in the barn. He took one (10), which is just slightly more than a quart. The tractor had run out of fuel one (11), or a little more than half a mile, from the barn.

Later I picked two (12) of apples. I probably gained a few (13) from all the apples I ate. Then I milked the cow. I filled four containers, each holding two pints or one (14). So I had one (15) in all.

Word Parts kilo-, centi-, milli-

Write a word to fit each meaning below.

kilo- means "one thousand"
centi- means "one-hundredth of"
milli- means "one-thousandth of"

16. one thousand meters
17. one one-hundredth of a meter
18. one one-thousandth of a meter
19. one one-hundredth of a liter

20. one thousand grams
21. one one-thousandth of a liter
22. one one-hundredth of a gram
23. one thousand liters

Measure Up Write the Core Word that belongs in the blank in each picture.

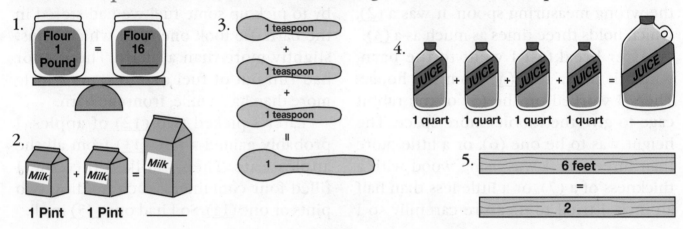

1. Flour 1 Pound = Flour 16 _____

2. Milk 1 Pint + Milk 1 Pint = Milk _____

3. 1 teaspoon + 1 teaspoon + 1 teaspoon = 1 _____

4. JUICE 1 quart + JUICE 1 quart + JUICE 1 quart + JUICE 1 quart = JUICE _____

5. 6 feet = 2 _____

Take a Close Look Write the Core Word that matches each clue.

6. It has a *c* and an *e* but no *n*.
7. It has an *e* and a *t* but no *m* and no *l*.
8. It has an *e* and a *u* but no *s*.

9. It has a double consonant but no *a*.
10. It has an *i* and an *r* but no *l*.

Break the Code Use the code to write each word.

Letter	b	e	h	i	k	l	m	n	o	r	s	t	u
Code	⊡	○	◪	■	⊠	△	◮	◨	⊗	◐	▲	□	●

11. ⊠■△⊗△○□○◐
12. ⊡●▲▲○△▲
13. △■□○○◐
14. ◮■□●□○▲
15. ◮○□○◐

Use the Dictionary Look up each underlined word in the dictionary.
Write the definition that shows how the word is used in the sentence.

16. Adam read the <u>minutes</u> at the meeting.
17. The music has an even <u>meter</u>.
18. The <u>volume</u> on the TV is too loud.

An inventory is a list of things on hand. Write an inventory of things you might find in a garage, basement, or other storage area. Use at least four Core Words from this lesson.

Proofreding prakticee

1–5. Here is a draft of the inventory that one student wrote. Find five misspelled words and write them correctly.

Basement Inventory

1. five yards of rope
2. a quort of motor oil
3. a timer that times up to sixty minites
4. a gallen of paint
5. boards one meter long and a centometer thick
6. grass seed for one aker of land

Now proofread your own inventory and correct any errors.

CORE			CHALLENGE
yards	teaspoon	meter	leagues
millimeter	ounces	minutes	eon
quart	gallon	volume	degree
acre	liter	tablespoon	decades
centimeter	bushels	kilometer	amperes

35 Spelling the Names of National Parks

CORE

1. Grand Canyon
2. Yosemite
3. Bryce Canyon
4. Grand Teton
5. Glacier Bay
6. Crater Lake
7. Everglades
8. Badlands
9. Petrified Forest
10. Acadia
11. Hawaii Volcanoes
12. Carlsbad Caverns
13. Mammoth Cave
14. Sequoia
15. Mount Rainier

CHALLENGE

16. parka
17. compass
18. canteen
19. adventure
20. equipment

Say the words. Listen for the vowel and consonant sounds.

Study the spelling. Look for familiar and unusual spelling patterns. How is the long *i* sound spelled in *Bryce Canyon?* How is the /sh/ sound spelled in *Glacier Bay?* How does each word begin?

Write the words.

1–10. Write the Core Words that are written as two separate words.

11–15. Write the Core Words that are written as a single word.

16–17. Write the Challenge Words that have three syllables.

18–20. Write the Challenge Words that have two syllables.

SPELLING TIP

The names of our national parks have many familiar spellings. Some unusual spellings must be remembered. All begin with capital letters.

Write the Core Words that best complete the story.

A Wealth of Wonders

The United States contains a wealth of national parks. In the East, visit the swamps of the (1) in Florida and the forests of (2) in Maine. Toward the middle of the country, go to see the rugged, barren (3) of South Dakota and Nebraska. If you like caves, go to see (4) in Kentucky and (5) in New Mexico.

While you are in the Southwest, stop in Arizona to gaze down the steep walls of the (6), then go to the (7) to see logs that have petrified, or turned to stone. Head north to Utah to see the odd-shaped, colorful rocks at (8). In Wyoming are the lovely mountains and forests of the (9).

In California are (10), where you will be amazed by the giant sequoia trees, and (11), which features jagged mountains and sparkling lakes. In Oregon, visit (12) and see the lake formed by the crater of a volcano. Then go north to Washington to view (13), the state's highest mountain. You will also love (14) in Alaska, where you can see glaciers and whales. Finally travel southwest across the Pacific Ocean to see the (15).

Compound Words

Badlands is a compound word. Write more compound words by adding each word to a word below. Use each word once.

moon	wood	water
rise	post	camp
humming	stick	pack

16. fire___   18. sun___   20. back___   22. match___   24. ___bird

17. ___site   19. ___card   21. ___light   23. ___fall

Solve the Puzzle

Figure out the missing letters and write the Core Words. Then use the letters above the trees to write what you find in national parks.

1. _ a _ _ _ _   _ _ _ _ a _ _ _ _

2. _ _ _ _ _ _ _ e _   _ _ _ e _ _
   🌲

3. _ _ _ t _ _ _ a _ _
   🌲

4. _ _ _ _ _ l _ _ _ _
   🌲

5. _ r _ _ _   _ _ o _
   🌲

6. _ _ a _ _ _ _   _ _ _
   🌲

7. _ _ _ n _ _ a _ _ _ _ _
   🌲

8. _ _ _ c _ _ a _ _ _ _
   🌲

9. _ _ _ l _ _ _ _   _ _ e _ _ _
   🌲

10. _ _ _ e _ _ _ _
    🌲

11. What do you find in national parks? _ _ _ _ _ _ _ _ _ _

Spot the Colors

Write the name of the national park that is printed in each color.

S A B E C A Q A D U D L I O A N I D A S A

12. red

13. blue

14. green

Use the Clues

Write the Core Word that fits each clue.

15. Which park name has three syllables and two short *a* sounds?

16. Which park name has a double consonant?

130   Lesson 35

WRITE ON YOUR OWN

An itinerary is a planned route of travel. Write an itinerary for a trip that you would like to take. Name each place you will visit and tell when you will be there. Use at least four Core Words from this lesson.

Proofreding prakticee
a — c

1-4. Here is a draft of the itinerary that one student wrote. Find four misspelled words and write them correctly.

> On June 24 I will arrive at Mount Ranier near Seattle Washington. I will camp there for three days, then travel south and arrive at Krater Lake in oregon on June 29. After two days, I will continue south to california where I will visit Sequoya and Yosemiti. I will be home on july 3.

5-8. The student who wrote this itinerary left out a comma between a city and state. He also forgot to capitalize three proper nouns. Copy his itinerary and correct the errors.

Now proofread your own itinerary and correct any errors.

CORE			CHALLENGE
Grand Canyon	Crater Lake	Hawaii Volcanoes	parka
Yosemite	Everglades	Carlsbad Caverns	compass
Bryce Canyon	Badlands	Mammoth Cave	canteen
Grand Teton	Petrified Forest	Sequoia	adventure
Glacier Bay	Acadia	Mount Rainier	equipment

36 REVIEW

Write a Core Word from Lesson 31 to complete each sentence. The missing word will rhyme with the underlined word and will have a silent letter.

1. Silly people are <u>joke</u> ___.

2. If you borrow money to buy a dog, you have a <u>pet</u> ___.

3. The hour for poetry is ___ <u>time</u>.

4. An uninterested weapon is a <u>bored</u> ___.

Write each phrase or sentence below. Replace the underlined word or words with a Core Word from Lesson 32. Each word will have the /f/ sound. The new phrase or sentence is a famous quotation.

5. "Anything awful makes me <u>show amusement</u>."

   —CHARLES LAMB

6. "I realize that patriotism is not <u>as much as is necessary</u>."

   —EDITH CAVELL

7. "She was a <u>ghost</u> of delight."

   —WILLIAM WORDSWORTH

8. "The harder the conflict, the more glorious the <u>victory</u>."

   —THOMAS PAINE

Write a Core Word from Lesson 33 that fits each group of words.

9. cup, ruler, teaspoon, ___

10. bump, bang, hit, ___

11. test, question, ___

12. talk, meeting, conversation, ___

Write a Core Word from Lesson 34 for each clue below. Each word you write will begin with the same letter as the underlined word.

13. The guests drank a ___ of grape juice.
14. The woman bought ___ of yarn!
15. The parking lot is an ___ of asphalt.
16. The farmer picked ___ of beets.

Write a Core Word from Lesson 35 by filling in the missing letters below.

17. ___ ___ ___ ___ ___ ___ b a d C a v e r n s
18. G r a n d T ___ ___ ___ ___ ___
19. H a w ___ ___ ___   V ___ l ___ a n ___ ___ ___
20. Y ___ s ___ ___ ___ ___ ___

Steps in the Writing Process

Here are some steps you might want to use to help you write.

1 **Prewriting**

Think about what you want to write about.

What have you done or seen?

What things do you remember?

Ask a friend for ideas.

Explore your topic.

Make a list of things that pop into your head.

Draw a picture or diagram of your idea.

Share your thoughts with others.

2 **Drafting**

Make a first try at writing your paper.

Write quickly to get your ideas down.

Do not worry about mistakes now.

3 Revising

Carefully read what you have written.

Change your words, sentences, or ideas to make them better.

Read your writing to someone else. Ask him or her how to make it better.

4 Proofreading

Read what you have written again.

Look for errors in spelling, capitalization, and punctuation, and correct them.

5 Publishing

Make a clean, neat copy of what you have written.
Be careful not to make new mistakes.

Add pictures, a title, or other special things.

Share your writing with others.

How to Use the Dictionary

The word you look up in a dictionary is called an **entry word**. A dictionary tells you how to spell and pronounce the word. It also gives one or more definitions for the word.

The entry words in a dictionary are arranged in alphabetical order. If two words have the same first letter, they are put in alphabetical order using the second letter.

Study the dictionary entries below. Notice how much you can learn about a word from a dictionary.

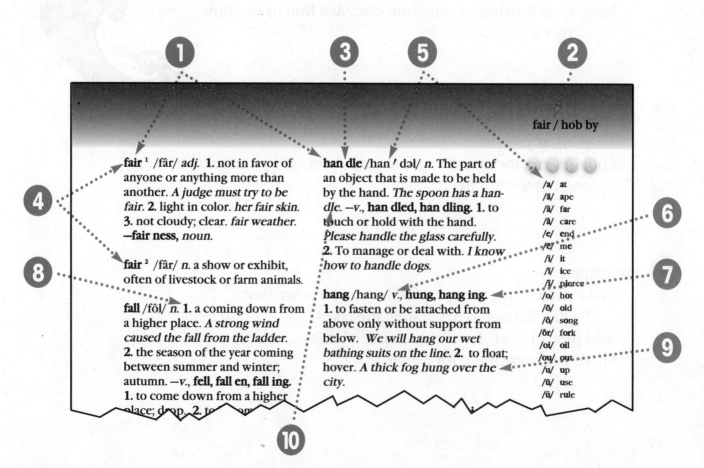

fair / hob by

fair [1] /fâr/ *adj.* **1.** not in favor of anyone or anything more than another. *A judge must try to be fair.* **2.** light in color. *her fair skin.* **3.** not cloudy; clear. *fair weather.* **—fair ness,** *noun.*

fair [2] /fâr/ *n.* a show or exhibit, often of livestock or farm animals.

fall /fôl/ *n.* **1.** a coming down from a higher place. *A strong wind caused the fall from the ladder.* **2.** the season of the year coming between summer and winter; autumn. **—v., fell, fall en, fall ing. 1.** to come down from a higher place; drop. **2.** t...

han dle /han ′ dəl/ *n.* The part of an object that is made to be held by the hand. *The spoon has a han-dle.* **—v., han dled, han dling. 1.** to touch or hold with the hand. *Please handle the glass carefully.* **2.** To manage or deal with. *I know how to handle dogs.*

hang /hang/ *v.,* **hung, hang ing. 1.** to fasten or be attached from above only without support from below. *We will hang our wet bathing suits on the line.* **2.** to float; hover. *A thick fog hung over the city.*

/a/	at
/ā/	ape
/ä/	far
/â/	care
/e/	end
/ē/	me
/i/	it
/ī/	ice
/î/	pierce
/o/	hot
/ō/	old
/ô/	song
/ôr/	fork
/oi/	oil
/ou/	out
/u/	up
/ū/	use
/ü/	rule

136

1 The **entry word** is the word you look up. Entry words are in bold type and listed in alphabetical order.

2 At the top of each dictionary page are two words called **guide words.** They are the first and last entry words appearing on that page. Guide words help you find an entry word quickly.

3 Words with more than one **syllable** are shown in two parts. A space separates the syllables.

4 Sometimes there is more than one entry for a word. When this happens, each entry is numbered.

5 After the entry word is the **pronunciation.** It is given between two lines. Special letters are used to show how to pronounce the the word. A **pronunciation key** shows the sound for each special letter. The pronunciation key is found on each page of the dictionary.

6 An abbreviation for the **part of speech** of the entry word is given after the pronunciation.

7 The dictionary also shows **irregular forms** of the entry word. If an *-s, -es, -ed,* or *-ing* is simply added to the word, the dictionary does not list these regularly spelled forms.

8 One or more **definitions** are given for each entry word. If there is more than one definition, the definitions are numbered.

9 Sometimes the entry word is used in a **sample sentence** or **phrase** to help explain the meaning of the entry word.

10 Some words can be more than one part of speech. If so, the dictionary sometimes gives another definition for the entry word.

Speller Dictionary

adj.   adjective
adv.   adverb
conj.   conjunction
contr. contraction
def.   definition
interj. interjection
n.   noun
pl.   plural
prep.   preposition
pron.   pronoun
sing.   singular
v.   verb
v.i.   intransitive verb
v.t.   transitive verb

a bove /ə buv ʹ/ *adv.* overhead. —*prep.* **1.** over or higher than. **2.** higher in rank. **3.** more than; over.

ab sent /ab ʹ sənt/ *adj.* not present; missing.

A ca di a /ə kā ʹ dē ə/ *n.* a National Park in Maine.

ac ci dent /ak ʹ si dənt/ *n.* something that happens for no apparent reason and is unexpected.

ac count /ə kount ʹ/ *n.* **1.** a spoken or written statement; report. **2.** a record of money spent or received. **3.** a sum of money that a person allows a bank to hold until it is needed. —*v.* to consider to be.

ache /āk/ *v.* **ached, ach ing. 1.** to hurt with a dull or constant pain. **2.** to want very much; be eager. —*n.* a dull or constant pain.

a cre /ā ʹ kər/ *n.* an area of land equal to 43,560 square feet.

ac tion /ak ʹ shən/ *n.* **1.** the process of doing something. **2.** a way of working or moving.

ac tor /ak ʹ tər/ *n.* a person who plays a part in a play, movie, television program, or radio program.

ac tress /ak ʹ tris/ *n., pl.* **actresses.** a girl or woman who plays a part in a play, movie, television program, or radio program.

a dore /ə dôr ʹ/ *v.* **a dored, a dor ing. 1.** to love and admire very much. **2.** to worship. **3.** to like something very much. *I adore rock music.*

ad ven ture /ad ven ʹ chər/ *n.* an exciting or unusual experience.

af ford /ə fôrd ʹ/ *v.* **1.** to have enough money to pay for. **2.** to be able to spare or give.

a gain /ə gen ʹ/ *adv.* once more; another time.

a gree /ə grē ʹ/ *v.* to have the same opinion or feeling.

air plane /âr ʹ plān ʹ/ *n.* a machine with wings that flies.

138

aisle /īl/ *n.* the space between two rows or sections of something.

-al a suffix used to form adjectives that means of, relating to, or characterized by. *Seasonal* means of a season.

al low ance /ə lou ′ əns/ *n.* a sum of money or quantity set aside for a particular reason.

a loud /ə loud ′/ *adv.* using the voice so as to be heard.

al pha bet /al ′ fə bet ′/ *n.* the letters or characters that are used to write a language, arranged in their proper order.

al though /ôl <u>th</u>ō ′/ *conj.* in spite of the fact that; though.

a mong /ə mung ′/ *prep.* **1.** in the middle of; surrounded by. **2.** in association with. *among friends.* **3.** with a portion or share for each of.

a mount /ə mount ′/ *n.* **1.** the sum of two or more numbers or quantities. **2.** quantity. *no amount of hard work.* —*v.* to be equal; be the same.

am pere /am ′ pîr/ *n.* the standard unit for measuring the strength of an electric current.

a muse /ə mūz ′/ *v.* **a mused**, **a mus ing**. **1.** to cause to laugh or smile. **2.** to entertain.

-ance a suffix used to form nouns from adjectives ending in *-ant* that means the state, quality, or condition of being. *brilliance.*

an chor /ang ′ kər/ *n.* **1.** a heavy, metal device that is attached to a ship by a chain or cable. **2.** any device that holds something in place. —*v.* **1.** to hold something in place with an anchor. **2.** to fasten firmly.

an gel /ān ′ jəl/ *n.* in the Bible and other writings, a heavenly being who serves God as a helper and messenger.

an gle /ang ′ gəl/ *n.* **1.** the figure formed by two lines or flat surfaces that extend from one point or line. **2.** a way of thinking or feeling about something; point of view. —*v.* **an gled**, **an gling**. to move or turn so as to form an angle.

an swer /an ′ sər/ *n.* **1.** something said or written in reply. **2.** the solution to a problem. —*v.* **1.** to speak or write as a reply. **2.** to agree with; match. *The suspect answers that description.*

an ti bi ot ic /an ′ tē bī ot ′ ik/ *n.* a drug that is used in medicine to kill or slow the growth of germs that cause disease.

an y one /en ′ ē wun ′/ *pron.* any person whatever; anybody.

ap par ent /ə par ′ ənt/ *adj.* **1.** easily seen or understood. **2.** seeming real or true even though it may not be. *the apparent size of a star.*

ap pen dix /ə pen ′ diks/ *n.*, *pl.* **ap pen dix es** or **ap pen di ces**. /ə pen ′ də sēz/ **1.** a short, hollow pouch that is attached to the large intestine. **2.** a section at the end of a book or other piece of writing.

/a/	at
/ā/	ape
/ä/	far
/â/	care
/e/	end
/ē/	me
/i/	it
/ī/	ice
/î/	pierce
/o/	hot
/ō/	old
/ô/	song
/ôr/	fork
/oi/	oil
/ou/	out
/u/	up
/ū/	use
/ü/	rule
/ù/	pull
/ûr/	turn
/ch/	chin
/ng/	sing
/sh/	shop
/th/	thin
/<u>th</u>/	this
/hw/	white
/zh/	treasure
/ə/	about
	taken
	pencil
	lemon
	circus

139

ap ple /ap ′ əl/ *n.* a round fruit with red, yellow, or green skin.

a pron /ā ′ prən/ *n.* a garment worn over the front of the body to protect one's clothing.

ar gu ment /är ′ gyə mənt/ *n.* a discussion of something by people who do not agree.

a rise /ə rīz ′/ *v.* **a rose, a ris en, a ris ing.** **1.** to move upward; rise. **2.** to come into being; appear. *Questions often arise in our minds as we read about new things.*

ar row head /ar ′ ō hed ′/ *n.* the pointed tip or head of an arrow.

ar ter y /är ′ tə rē/ *n., pl.* **ar ter ies.** **1.** one of the blood vessels that carries blood away from the heart. **2.** a main road or channel.

ar tist /är ′ tist/ *n.* a person whose work shows talent or skill.

-ary a suffix that means a person or thing connected with; of. *Missionary* means of a mission.

a sleep /ə slēp ′/ *adj.* **1.** not awake; sleeping. **2.** without feeling; numb. —*adv.* into a condition of sleep.

as phalt /as ′ fôlt/ *n.* a brown or black substance found in the ground or obtained when petroleum is refined.

as sist ant /ə sis ′ tənt/ *n.* a person who assists; helper. —*adj.* acting to assist another person.

as tound /ə stound ′/ *v.* to surprise very much; amaze; astonish.

as tro naut /as ′ trə nôt ′/ *n.* a person trained to fly in an aircraft.

ath lete /ath ′ lēt/ *n.* a person who is trained in sports or other exercises that take strength, skill, and speed.

au to mo bile /ô ′ tə mə bēl ′/ *n.* a vehicle that usually has four wheels and is powered by an engine that uses gasoline; car.

au tumn /ô ′ təm/ *n.* the season of the year coming between summer and winter; fall.

a ward /ə wôrd ′/ *v.* **1.** to give after careful thought. **2.** to give because of a legal decision. —*n.* something that is given after careful thought.

aw ful /ô ′ fəl/ *adj.* causing fear, dread, or awe; terrible.

• • • **B** • • • • • • • • • • • • •

ba by /bā ′ bē/ *n., pl.* **ba bies.** **1.** a very young child; infant. **2.** the youngest person in a family or group. **3.** a person who acts in a childish way. —*adj.* **1.** of or for a baby. **2.** very young. —*v.* **ba bied, ba by ing.** to treat like a baby.

back pack /bak ′ pak ′/ *n.* a bag that is used to carry things on the back. —*v.*

to go hiking or camping while carrying a backpack.

badge /baj/ *n.* something worn to show that a person belongs to a certain group or has received an honor.

Bad lands /bad ′ landz ′/ *n.* a national park in southwestern South Dakota.

bal lad /bal ′ əd/ *n.* a single poem or song that tells a story.

bal lot /bal ′ ət/ *n.* a printed form or other object used in voting.

bar be cue /bär ′ bi kū ′/ *n.* **1.** a meal cooked outdoors over an open fire. **2.** a grill or small fireplace that uses gas or charcoal for fuel. —*v.* **bar be cued**, **bar be cu ing**. to cook a meal outdoors over an open fire.

bare foot /bâr ′ füt ′/ *adj.* having the feet bare. —*adv.* with the feet bare.

bar gain /bär ′ gin/ *n.* **1.** something offered for sale or bought at a low price. **2.** an agreement.

bar rel /bar ′ əl/ *n.* **1.** a large, round, wooden container with curved sides. **2.** a metal tube that forms part of a gun.

bat tle /bat ′ əl/ *n.* **1.** a fight between two armed persons or groups. **2.** a long, hard effort or contest; struggle. —*v.* **bat tled**, **bat tling**. to fight or struggle.

bea ver /bē ′ vər/ *n.* a furry, brown animal that has a broad, flat tail and webbed hind feet to help it swim.

be cause /bi kôz ′/ *conj.* for the reason that.

be come /bi kum ′/ *v.* **be came**, **be come**, **be com ing**. —*v.* **1.** to grow to be; come to be. **2.** to look good on; flatter. *That suit becomes you.*

bed spread /bed ′ spred ′/ *n.* a top cover for a bed.

be gin /bi gin ′/ *v.* **be gan**, **be gun**, **be gin ning**. **1.** to make a start. **2.** to come into being. *Spring begins in March.*

be have /bi hāv ′/ *v.* **be haved**, **be hav ing**. *v.* to do things in a certain way, act.

be hind /bi hīnd ′/ *prep.* **1.** at the back of. **2.** later than; after. **3.** in support of; backing. *The whole town got behind the plan.*

beige /bāzh/ *n.* a pale brown color —*adj.* having the color beige.

be lieve /bi lēv ′/ *v.* **be lieved**, **be liev ing**. to feel sure that something is true, real, or worthwhile.

be long /bi lông ′/ *v.* **1.** to have a special or right place. **2.** to be owned by someone. **3.** to be a member.

bench /bench/ *n., pl.* **bench es**. **1.** a long seat. **2.** the position or job of a judge in a court of law.

be neath /bi nēth ′/ *prep.* **1.** lower than; below; under. **2.** unworthy of. —*adv.* in a lower place; below.

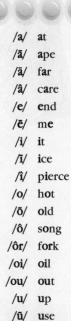

/a/	at
/ā/	ape
/ä/	far
/â/	care
/e/	end
/ē/	me
/i/	it
/ī/	ice
/î/	pierce
/o/	hot
/ō/	old
/ô/	song
/ôr/	fork
/oi/	oil
/ou/	out
/u/	up
/ū/	use
/ü/	rule
/ù/	pull
/ûr/	turn
/ch/	chin
/ng/	sing
/sh/	shop
/th/	thin
/th/	this
/hw/	white
/zh/	treasure
/ə/	about
	taken
	pencil
	lemon
	circus

be side /bi sīd ′/ *prep.* **1.** at the side of; next to. **2.** not connected with.

be stow /bi stō ′/ *v.* to give.

be tray /bi trā ′/ *v.* to be unfaithful to.

be tween /bi twēn ′/ *prep.* **1.** in the space or time separating. **2.** joining. **3.** involving, among. **4.** by comparing. *You can choose between pancakes and oatmeal. —adv.* in the space or time separating two things.

be wil der /bi wil ′ dər/ *v.* to confuse or puzzle; mix up.

be witch / bi wich ′/ *v.* **1.** to cast a spell over someone using magic. **2.** to charm.

be yond /bē ond ′, bi yond ′/ *prep.* **1.** on the far side of. **2.** later than. **3.** outside the reach or limits of; too advanced for. *—adv.* farther on.

bike /bīk/ *n.* a bicycle. *—v.* **biked**, **bik ing**. to ride a bicycle.

birth place /bûrth ′ plās ′/ *n.* the place where a person was born.

bis cuit /bis ′ kit/ *n.*, pl. **bis cuits**, **bis cuit**. **1.** a small cake of baked dough. **2.** a cracker.

blan ket /blang ′ kit/ *n.* **1.** a covering made of material. **2.** anything that covers like a blanket. *a blanket of fog.*

blis ter /blis ′ tər/ *n.* a sore place on the skin that looks like a small bubble.

bliz zard /bliz ′ ərd/ *n.* a heavy snowstorm with very strong winds.

blood hound /blud ′ hound ′/ *n.* a large dog with long, drooping ears and a wrinkled face.

blood stream /blud ′ strēm ′/ *n.* the blood flowing through the body.

blouse /blous, blouz/ *n.* a loose piece of clothing for the upper part of the body.

blue print /blü ′ print ′/ *n.* a paper showing white lines on a blue background, used to show the plan for building something.

board /bôrd/ *n.* **1.** a long, flat piece of wood used for a special purpose. **2.** a group of people who are chosen to manage or direct something. **3.** meals served daily to guests for pay. *—v.* **1.** to cover with boards. **2.** to pay for as room to sleep in and meals. **3.** to get on a ship, plane, or train.

boast /bōst/ *v.* **1.** to brag about oneself. **2.** to be proud of having. *—n.* a statement in which one brags.

bod y guard /bod ′ ē gärd ′/ *n.* a person or persons who protect someone from danger or attack.

bone /bōn/ *n.* one of the parts of the skeleton of an animal with a backbone. *—v.* **boned**, **bon ing**. to take out the bones of.

bot tle /bot ′ əl/ *n.* a container to hold liquids. *—v.* to put in bottles. **bot tler**, *n.* **bot tled**, **bot tling**.

adj.	adjective
adv.	adverb
conj.	conjunction
contr.	contraction
def.	definition
interj.	interjection
n.	noun
pl.	plural
prep.	preposition
pron.	pronoun
sing.	singular
v.	verb
v.i.	intransitive verb
v.t.	transitive verb

bough /bou/ *n.* a large branch of a tree.

bought /bôt/ *v.* past tense and past participle of *buy.*

boul der /bōl ʹ dər/ *n.* a large, usually rounded rock.

brain /brān/ *n.* the large mass of nerve tissues that is inside the skull of persons and animals.

brake /brāk/ *n.* a device used to stop or slow down the movement of a vehicle. —*v.* **braked, brak ing.** to cause something to stop or slow down by using a brake.

break /brāk/ *v.* **broke, bro ken, break ing. 1.** to come apart by force. **2.** to crack a bone. **3.** to stop; end. **4.** to surpass. *to break a record.* **5.** to fail to obey. *Don't break the law.* **6.** to fill with sorrow. **7.** to tell; reveal. —*n.* **1.** a broken place. **2.** a sudden change. **3.** a short rest period.

breath /breth/ *n.* **1.** air drawn in and forced out of the lungs when you breathe. **2.** the act of breathing. **3.** the ability to breathe easily. **4.** a slight flow of air.

bridge /brij/ *n.* **1.** a structure built across a river, road, or railroad track so that people can get from one side to the other. **2.** the top, bony part of a person's nose. **3.** a raised structure on the deck of a ship. —*v.* **bridged, bridg ing.** to build a bridge across.

brief /brēf/ *adj.* **1.** short in time. **2.** using few words. —*v.* to give important details or facts to.

bring /bring/ *v.* **brought, bring ing.** to cause something or someone to come with you.

bris tle /bris ʹ əl/ *n.* a short, stiff hair. —*v.* **bris tled, bris tling.** to stand up stiffly.

broad /brôd/ *adj.* **1.** large from one side to the other. **2.** wide in range; not limited. **3.** clear and open.

bro ken /brō ʹ kən/ *v.* past participle of *break.* —*adj.* **1.** in pieces. **2.** not kept. **3.** not working; damaged. **4.** not spoken perfectly. *broken English.*

brought /brôt/ *v.* past tense and past participle of *bring.*

browse /browz/ *v.* **browsed, brows ing. 1.** to look through something casually. **2.** to feed or nibble on the leaves or twigs of a tree or shrub.

bruise /brüz/ *n.* **1.** an injury that does not break the skin but makes a bluish or blackish mark on it. **2.** a mark on a fruit, vegetable, or plant caused by a blow or bump.

Bryce Can yon /brīs kan ʹ yən/ *n.* a national park in southern Utah.

bub ble /bub ʹ əl/ *n.* a small, round body of air or other gas, usually in or on the surface of a liquid. —*v.* **bub bled, bub bling.** to form bubbles.

build /bild/ *v.* **built, build ing. 1.** to make by putting parts or materials together. **2.** to form little by little; develop. —*n.* the way in which someone is put together. *a strong build.*

/a/	at
/ā/	ape
/ä/	far
/â/	care
/e/	end
/ē/	me
/i/	it
/ī/	ice
/î/	pierce
/o/	hot
/ō/	old
/ô/	song
/ôr/	fork
/oi/	oil
/ou/	out
/u/	up
/ū/	use
/ü/	rule
/ù/	pull
/ûr/	turn
/ch/	chin
/ng/	sing
/sh/	shop
/th/	thin
/th/	this
/hw/	white
/zh/	treasure
/ə/	about
	taken
	pencil
	lemon
	circus

built /bilt/ *v.* past tense and past participle of *build*.

bum ble bee /bum ′ bəl bē ′/ *n.* a large bee with a thick, hairy body.

bun dle /bun ′ dəl/ *n.* a number of things tied or wrapped together. —*v.* **bun dled, bun dling.** to tie or wrap together.

bur den /bûr ′ dən/ *n.* **1.** something that is carried. **2.** something very hard to bear. —*v.* to put too heavy a load on.

adj.	adjective
adv.	adverb
conj.	conjunction
contr.	contraction
def.	definition
interj.	interjection
n.	noun
pl.	plural
prep.	preposition
pron.	pronoun
sing.	singular
v.	verb
v.i.	intransitive verb
v.t.	transitive verb

burnt /bûrnt/ *v.* a past tense and a past participle of *burn*.

burst /bûrst/ *v.* **1.** to break open suddenly. **2.** to be very full. **3.** to come or go suddenly. **4.** to show strong, sudden emotion. —*n.* **1.** the act of bursting. **2.** a sudden effort.

bush el /bùsh ′ əl/ *n.* a measure for grain, fruit, vegetables, and other dry things.

busi ness /biz ′ nis/ *n., pl.* **busi ness es.** **1.** the work that a person does to earn a living. **2.** matters or affairs. *Don't meddle in other people's business.*

bus y /biz ′ ē/ *adj.* **bus i er, bus i est.** **1.** doing something; active. **2.** full of activity. **3.** in use. —*v.* to make busy; keep busy.

buy /bī/ *v.* **bought, buy ing.** to get something by paying money for it;

purchase. —*n.* something offered for sale at a low price; bargain.

buy er /bī ′ ər/ *n.* a person who buys.

cab in /kab ′ in/ *n.* **1.** a small, simple house. **2.** private room on a ship. **3.** a place in an aircraft for passengers, crew members, and cargo.

cab i net /kab ′ ə nit/ *n.* **1.** a piece of furniture that has shelves or drawers. **2.** a group of people who give advice to the leader of a nation.

ca ble /kā ′ bəl/ *n.* **1.** a strong, thick rope. **2.** a bundle of wires that has a covering around it for protection. **3.** a message that is sent under the ocean by cable. —*v.* **ca bled, ca bling.** to send a message by cable.

cam er a /kam ′ ər ə, kam ′ rə/ *n.* a device for taking photographs or motion pictures.

cam paign /kam pān ′/ *n.* a series of actions that are planned and carried out to bring about a particular result.

can cel /kan ′ səl/ *v.* **can celed, can cel ing.** **1.** to decide not to do; call off. **2.** to cross off or mark a line through to show that it cannot be used again.

can teen /kan tēn ′/ *n.* **1.** a small, metal container for carrying water or other liquids to drink. **2.** a store in a school or factory that sells food and drinks.

can yon /kan ′ yən/ *n.* a deep valley with very high, steep sides.

cap tain /kap ′ tən/ *n.* a person who is the leader of a group. —*v.* to be the captain of; lead.

Carls bad Cav erns /kärlz ′ bad kav ′ ərnz/ *n.* underground caves in southeastern New Mexico.

car pet /kär ′ pit/ *n.* a covering for a floor. —*v.* to cover with a carpet.

car ton /kär ′ tən/ *n.* a box or container that is made of cardboard, paper, or other materials.

car toon /kär tün ′/ *n.* a drawing that shows people or things in a way that makes you laugh.

cas se role /kas ′ ə rōl ′/ *n.* **1.** a deep dish in which food can be cooked and served. **2.** food prepared in such a dish.

cas tle /kas ′ əl/ *n.* a large building or group of buildings having high, thick walls with towers.

cat a log /kat ′ ə lôg ′, kat ′ ə log ′/ also, **cat a logue**, *n.* a list. —*v.* to make a list of; put in a list.

catch /kach/ *v.* **caught, catch ing. 1.** to take or get hold of something or someone that is moving. **2.** to get, receive. —*n., pl.* **catch es. 1.** the act of catching something or someone. **2.** something that is caught. **3.** a game in which a ball is thrown back and forth between the players. **4.** a hidden reason or condition; trick.

caught /kôt/ *v.* past tense and past participle of *catch.*

cause /kôz/ *n.* **1.** a person or thing that makes something happen. **2.** something a person or group believes in. —*v.* **caused, caus ing.** to make something happen.

ce ment /sə ment ′/ *n.* **1.** a powder that is made by burning a mixture of limestone and clay. **2.** any soft, sticky substance that hardens to make things hold together. —*v.* **1.** to cover with cement or concrete. **2.** to make firm or secure.

cent /sent/ *n.* a coin of the United States and Canada. One hundred cents is equal to one dollar.

cen ti me ter /sen ′ tə mē ′ ter/ *n.* a unit of length in the metric system. One inch equals about two and a half centimeters.

cen ti pede /sen ′ tə pēd ′/ *n.* a small animal that has a long body divided into many segments.

cen tur y /sen ′ chə rē/ *n., pl.* **cen tu ries.** a period of one hundred years.

/a/	at
/ā/	ape
/ä/	far
/â/	care
/e/	end
/ē/	me
/i/	it
/ī/	ice
/î/	pierce
/o/	hot
/ō/	old
/ô/	song
/ôr/	fork
/oi/	oil
/ou/	out
/u/	up
/ū/	use
/ü/	rule
/ù/	pull
/ûr/	turn
/ch/	chin
/ng/	sing
/sh/	shop
/th/	thin
/th/	this
/hw/	white
/zh/	treasure
/ə/	about
	taken
	pencil
	lemon
	circus

ce re al /sîr ′ ē əl/ *n.* **1.** any grass whose grains are used for food. **2.** a food that is made from this grain.

choose /chüz/ *v.* **chose, cho sen. 1.** to pick. **2.** to decide or prefer to do something.

chord [1] /kôrd/ *n.* combination of three or more notes of music that are sounded at the same time to produce a harmony.

chord [2] /kôrd/ *n.* a straight line that connects any two points on the circumference of a circle.

chow der /chow ′ dər/ *n.* a thick soup made with fish or clams and vegetables.

chuck le /chuk ′ əl/ *v.* **chuck led, chuck ling.** to laugh in a quiet way. —*n.* a quiet laugh.

churn /chûrn/ *n.* a container in which cream or milk is shaken or beaten to make butter.

adj.	adjective
adv.	adverb
conj.	conjunction
contr.	contraction
def.	definition
interj.	interjection
n.	noun
pl.	plural
prep.	preposition
pron.	pronoun
sing.	singular
v.	verb
v.i.	intransitive verb
v.t.	transitive verb

cit i zen /sit ′ ə zən/ *n.* **1.** a person who was born in a country or who chooses to live in and become a member of a country. **2.** any person who lives in a town or city.

claim /klam/ *v.* **1.** to declare or take as one's own. **2.** to say that something is true. **3.** to take up; require; copy. —*n.* **1.** a demand for something as one's right. **2.** a statement that something is true.

clas si fy /klas ′ ə fī ′/ *v.* **clas si fied, clas si fy ing. 1.** to arrange in groups. **2.** to assign to a class.

clean /klēn/ *adj.* **1.** free from dirt. **2.** honorable or fair. **3.** complete; thorough. —*adv.* completely. —*v.* to make clean.

cliff /klif/ *n.* a high, steep face of rock or earth.

cli mate /klī ′ mit/ *n.* the average weather conditions of a place or region throughout the year.

climb /klīm/ *v.* **1.** to move upward or in some other direction over, across, or through something, using the hands and feet. **2.** to go steadily upward.

clin ic /klin ′ ik/ *n.* a place where medical care is given to people who do not need to stay in a hospital.

cloth ing /klō ′ <u>th</u>ing/ *n.* things worn to cover the body; cover.

clo ver /klō ′ vər/ *n.* a small plant having leaves made up of three leaflets and rounded, fragrant flower heads of white, red, or purple flowers.

clue /klü/ *n.* a hint that helps solve a problem or mystery.

clum sy /klum ′ zē/ *adj.* **clum si er, clum si est. 1.** awkward; not graceful. **2.** poorly made or done. —**clum si ly,** *adv.*

col lar / kol ′ ər/ *n.* a band or strap that is worn around the neck. —*v.* **1.** to put a collar on. **2.** to seize; capture.

col li sion /kə lizh ′ ən/ *n.* the act of colliding; a crash.

col o ny /kol ′ ə nē/ *n., pl.* **col o nies**. *n.* **1.** a group of people who settle in another land. **2.** a territory that is ruled by another country. **3.** a group of animals or plants of the same kind that live together.

col umn /kol ′ əm/ *n.* **1.** an upright structure shaped like a post; pillar. **2.** a part of a newspaper written regularly by one person. **3.** a long row or line.

comb /kōm/ *n.* **1.** a piece of plastic, metal, or other material that has a row of teeth. **2.** a thick, fleshy red crest on the head of chickens and other birds. —*v.* **1.** to smooth or arrange with a comb. **2.** to look everywhere; search thoroughly.

com bine /*v.* kəm bīn ′, *n.* kom ′ bīn/ *v.* **com bined**, **com bin ing**. to join together; unite. —*n.* a farm machine that harvests and threshes grain.

com et /kom ′ it/ *n.* a bright heavenly body made up of ice, frozen gases, and dust particles, and having a long visible tail.

com ment /kom ′ ent/ *n.* a remark or note. —*v.* to make a comment; remark.

com mon /kom ′ ən/ *adj.* **1.** happening often; familiar; usual. **2.** belonging equally to all. **3.** ordinary; average.

com mo tion /kə mō ′ shən/ *n.* a noisy confusion; disorder.

com pass /kum ′ pəs/ *n., pl.* **com pass es**. **1.** an instrument for showing directions. **2.** an instrument for drawing circles or measuring distances.

con demn /kən dem ′/ *v.* **1.** to express strong opposition to; disapprove of. **2.** to order as a punishment. **3.** to declare to be no longer safe or fit for use.

con fi dent /kon ′ fi dənt/ *adj.* having trust or faith; sure. —**confidently**, *adv.*

con gress /kong ′ gris/ *n., pl.* **con gress es**. **1.** an assembly of people who make laws. **2. Congress**. a branch of the government of the United States that makes laws.

con struc tion /kən struk ′ shən/ *n.* the act of constructing something; building.

corps /kôr/ *n., pl.* **corps** /kôrz/. **1.** a group of soldiers trained for special service. **2.** a group of persons who act or work together.

cor ral /kə ral ′, kôr al ′/ *n.* an area with a fence around it. —*v., pl.* **cor ralled**, **cor ral ling**. **1.** to drive or put into a corral. **2.** to get control or hold of by surrounding or gathering.

/a/	at
/ā/	ape
/ä/	far
/â/	care
/e/	end
/ē/	me
/i/	it
/ī/	ice
/î/	pierce
/o/	hot
/ō/	old
/ô/	song
/ôr/	fork
/oi/	oil
/ou/	out
/u/	up
/ū/	use
/ü/	rule
/ù/	pull
/ûr/	turn
/ch/	chin
/ng/	sing
/sh/	shop
/th/	thin
/th/	this
/hw/	white
/zh/	treasure
/ə/	about
	taken
	pencil
	lemon
	circus

could n't /kùd ′ ənt/ *contr.* shortened form of "could not."

coun try /kun ′ trē/ *n., pl.* **coun tries**. 1. any area of land; region. 2. an area of land that has boundaries and a government; nation. 3. the people of a nation. 4. the land outside of cities and towns. —*adj.* having to do with land outside of cities and towns; rural.

cour te sy /kûr ′ tə sē/ *n., pl.* **cour te sies**. 1. a way of behaving that shows good manners; politeness. 2. a polite and thoughtful act; favor.

court yard /kôrt ′ yärd ′/ *n.* an open area that is surrounded by walls or buildings.

cou sin /kuz ′ in/ *n.* the son or daughter of an aunt or uncle.

cov er /kuv ′ ər/ *v.* 1. to put something over or upon. 2. to be over the suface of 3. to hide from view. 4. to protect against loss or harm. 5. to travel or pass over. 6. to aim a firearm or other weapon at. 7. to get the details of; report. 8. to be enough.

cow ard /kou ′ ərd/ *n.* a person who lacks courage.

Cra ter Lake /krā ′ tər lak/ *n.* a national park in southwestern Oregon.

crawl /krôl/ *v.* 1. to move very slowly. 2. to be covered or feel as if covered with crawling things. —*n.* 1. a very slow movement. 2. a fast swimming stroke.

cred it /kred ′ it/ *n.* 1. belief in truth of something. 2. reputation. 3. praise or honor. 4. trust in a person to pay a debt later. 5. something that is owed to a person. —*v.* 1. to believe; trust. 2. to put an amount of money that is owed to someone into an account for that person.

croc o dile /krok ′ ə dīl ′/ *n.* a long animal with short legs, thick, scaly skin, and a long, strong tail.

crouch /krouch/ *v.* to stoop or bend low with the knees bent. —*n.* **crouches**.the act or position of crouching.

cru el /krü ′ əl/ *adj.* causing pain or suffering. —**cru el ly**, *adv.* —**cru el ness**, *n.*

cruise /krüz/ *v.* **cruised, cruis ing**. 1. to sail from place to place. 2. to move or ride from place to place.

crumb /krum/ *n.* tiny piece of bread, cake, cracker, or cookie.

cry stal /kris ′ təl/ *n.* 1. a clear kind of rock. 2. a body that is formed by certain substances when they change into a solid. 3. a very fine, clear glass used to make drinking glasses, bowls, plates, and vases. 4. the transparent covering that protects the face of a watch. —*adj.* 1. made of crystal. 2. like crystal; clear. *crystal water.*

cur rent /kûr ′ ənt/ *adj.* 1. belonging to the present time. 2. commonly used or accepted. —*n.* 1. a part of the air or of a body of water that is

adj.	adjective
adv.	adverb
conj.	conjunction
contr.	contraction
def.	definition
interj.	interjection
n.	noun
pl.	plural
prep.	preposition
pron.	pronoun
sing.	singular
v.	verb
v.i.	intransitive verb
v.t.	transitive verb

moving along in a path. **2.** a flow of electricity. **3.** the way events or thoughts seem to move along a path; trend. *the current of public opinion.*

cur tain /kûr ′ tin/ *n.* **1.** a piece of cloth hung across an open space. **2.** anything that screens or covers like a curtain. —*v.* to put a curtain over; screen.

cus tom er /kus ′ tə mər/ *n.* a person who buys something at a store or uses the services of a business establishment.

●●●**D**●●●●●●●●●●●●●●● ●●●

dan ger /dān ′ jer/ *n.* **1.** the chance that something bad or harmful will happen. **2.** something that may cause harm or injury.

debt /det/ *n.* **1.** something that is owed to another. **2.** the condition of owing.

dec ade /dek ′ ād/ *n.* a period of ten years.

de gree /di grē ′/ *n.* **1.** a stage or step in a process or series. **2.** amount or extent. **3.** a title given by a school or college for the completion of a course of study. **4.** a unit for measuring temperature. **5.** a unit for measuring angles or arcs.

de pen dent /di pen ′ dənt/ *adj.* **1.** relying on someone else for what

is needed or wanted. **2.** determined by how something else turns out. —*n.* a person whose home, food, and other basic needs are provided by someone else. —**de pen dent ly**. *adv.*

de stroy /di ′ stroi ′/ *v.* to ruin completely; wreck.

di a ry /dī ′ ə rē/ *n., pl.* **di a ries**. a written record of the things that one has done or thought each day.

dif fer ent /dif ′ ər ənt, dif ′ rənt/ *adj.* **1.** not alike or similar. **2.** not the same; separate. —**dif fer ent ly**, *adv.*

di rec tion /di rek ′ shən, dī rek ′ shən/ *n.* **1.** management or control; guidance. **2.** the line or course along which something moves, faces, or lies. **3.** an order or instruction on how to do something or how to act.

di rec tor /di rek ′ tər/ *n.* a person who supervises and guides the performers in a play, movie, or other performance.

dis- a prefix that means **1.** not or opposite. *Disapprove* means not to approve. **2.** lack of. *Disrespect* means lack of respect.

dis a gree /dis ′ ə grē ′/ *v.* **dis a greed**, **dis a gree ing**. **1.** to differ in opinion. **2.** to be different or unlike. **3.** to cause indigestion or discomfort.

dis ap pear /dis ′ ə pîr ′/ *v.* **1.** to go out of sight. **2.** to stop existing; become extinct.

/a/	at
/ā/	ape
/ä/	far
/â/	care
/e/	end
/ē/	me
/i/	it
/ī/	ice
/î/	pierce
/o/	hot
/ō/	old
/ô/	song
/ôr/	fork
/oi/	oil
/ou/	out
/u/	up
/ū/	use
/ü/	rule
/ù/	pull
/ûr/	turn
/ch/	chin
/ng/	sing
/sh/	shop
/th/	thin
/th/	this
/hw/	white
/zh/	treasure
/ə/	about
	taken
	pencil
	lemon
	circus

dis ap point / dis ′ ə point ′/ *v.* to fail to live up to the hopes of. —**dis ap point ed**, *adj.*

dis con nect /dis ′ kə nekt ′/ *v.* to separate from another part or from a source of electricity; break the connection of.

dis cov er /dis kuv ′ ər/ *v.* **1.** to see or find out for the first time. **2.** to notice; come upon.

dis cus sion /di skush ′ ən/ *n.* the act of talking something over; a serious exchange of opinions.

adj.	adjective
adv.	adverb
conj.	conjunction
contr.	contraction
def.	definition
interj.	interjection
n.	noun
pl.	plural
prep.	preposition
pron.	pronoun
sing.	singular
v.	verb
v.i.	intransitive verb
v.t.	transitive verb

dis grace /dis grās ′/ *n.* **1.** the loss of honor or respect: shame. **2.** a person or thing that causes a loss of honor or respect. —*v.* **dis graced**, **dis grac ing**. to bring shame to.

dis hon est /dis on ′ ist/ *adj.* not fair or honest. **dis hon est ly**. *adv.*

dis loy al /dis loi ′ əl/ *adj.* not loyal, unfaithful. —**dis loy al ly**, *adv.*

dis please /dis plēz ′/ *v.* **dis pleased**, **dis pleas ing**. to make dissatisfied or annoyed; disappoint.

dis trust /dis trust ′/ *v.* to have no trust or confidence in.

dol phin /dol ′ fin/ *n.* a sea animal that has two flippers and a snout that is like a beak.

don key /dong ′ kē, dung ′ kē/ *n.* a tame ass.

door bell /dôr ′ bel ′/ *n.* a bell or buzzer that is rung by someone who is outside a door.

doubt /dout/ *v.* **1.** to be uncertain about; not believe or trust fully. **2.** to think of as highly unlikely. —*n.* **1.** a feeling of not believing or trusting. **2.** a state of being undecided or unsure.

doz en /duz ′ ən/ *n., pl.* **doz ens**, **dozen**. a group of twelve.

draft /draft/ *n.* **1.** a current of air in an enclosed space. **2.** a device that controls the flow of air in something. **3.** a sketch, plan, or rough copy of something written.

draw bridge /drô ′ brij ′/ *n.* a kind of bridge that can be raised or moved so that ships can pass under it.

drift /drift/ *v.* **1.** to move because of a current of air or water. **2.** to pile up in masses from the action of the wind. **3.** to move from place to place without a goal or purpose. —*n.* **1.** movement caused by a current of air or water. **2.** something that has been moved along or piled up by air or water currents.

driz zle /driz ′ əl/ *v.* **driz zled**, **driz zling**. to rain steadily in fine, misty drops. —*n.* a fine, misty rain.

drop /drop/ *v.* **dropped** or **dropt**, **drop ping**. **1.** to fall or cause to fall to a lower position, move or fall down. **2.** to go into a less active position. **3.** to stop talking about or pursuing. *I* *decided to drop the subject.* **4.** to pay a casual, unplanned visit. **5.** to let out of a vehicle. **6.** to leave out; omit. —*n.* **1.** a very small amount of liquid. **2.** the act of dropping or falling. **3.** the distance between one thing and another below it.

dy na mo /dī ′ nə mō ′/ *n.* an electric motor or generator.

· · · E · · · · · · · · · · · · · · · · ·

earth quake /ûrth ′ kwāk ′/ *n.* a shaking or trembling of the ground.

earth worm /ûrth ′ wûrm ′/ *n.* a common worm made up of many round segments.

ech o /ek ′ ō/ *n., pl.* **ech oes.** the repeating of a sound. —*v.* **1.** to send back the sound of something. **2.** to be heard again. **3.** to repeat or imitate closely.

e di tion /i dish ′ ən/ *n.* **1.** the form in which a book is printed. *paperback edition.* **2.** the total number of copies of a book, newspaper, or magazine printed at one time. **3.** one of the copies of a book, newspaper, or magazine printed at one time.

ef fi cient /i fish ′ ənt/ *adj.* able to get results wanted with a minimum of time and effort. —**ef fi cient ly,** *adv.*

e lec tric i ty /i lek tris ′ i tē/ *n.* **1.** one of the basic forms of energy. **2.** electric current.

el e phant /el ′ ə fənt/ *n., pl.* **el e phants** or **el e phant.** a huge, gray animal with a long trunk, large, floppy ears, and two ivory tusks.

en- a prefix that means to cause to be or be like; make. *Enforce* means to cause to be in force.

-ence a suffix used to form nouns from adjectives ending in *-ent* that means the action, quality, state, or condition of being. *independence.*

en e my /en ′ ə mē/ *n., pl.* **en e mies.** **1.** a person or group of people who hates or wishes to harm another. **2.** a country that is at war with another country. **3.** something that is dangerous or harmful.

e nough /i nuf ′/ *adj.* as much or as many as needed. —*n.* an amount that is as much or as many as needed. —*adv.* to an amount or degree that is wanted or needed.

e on /ē ′ ən, ē ′ on/ *n.* a very long period of time.

ep i der mis /ep ′ i dùr ′ mis/ *n.* a protective outer layer of the skin. —**ep i der mal,** *adj.*

e quip ment /i kwip ′ mənt/ *n.* **1.** anything that is provided for a particular purpose or use; supplies. **2.** the act of equipping.

/a/	at
/ā/	ape
/ä/	far
/â/	care
/e/	end
/ē/	me
/i/	it
/ī/	ice
/î/	pierce
/o/	hot
/ō/	old
/ô/	song
/ôr/	fork
/oi/	oil
/ou/	out
/u/	up
/ū/	use
/ü/	rule
/ù/	pull
/ûr/	turn
/ch/	chin
/ng/	sing
/sh/	shop
/th/	thin
/th/	this
/hw/	white
/zh/	treasure
/ə/	about
	taken
	pencil
	lemon
	circus

151

-er [1] a suffix that means more. *Colder* means more cold than.

-er [2] a suffix that means one who does something. A *teacher* is a person who teaches.

e soph a gus / i sof ′ ə gəs/ *n.,* *pl.* **e soph a gi** /i sof ′ ə jī ′/ *n.* the muscular tube through which food moves from the throat to the stomach.

-est a suffix that means most. *Coldest* means the most cold.

es ti ma tion /es ′ tə mā ′ shən/ *n.* an opinion or judgment.

Ev er glades /Ev ′ ər glādz ′/ *n.* a national park in south Florida.

eve ry where /ev ′ rē wâr ′/ *adv.* in every place; in all places.

ev i dent /ev ′ i dənt/ *adj.* easily seen or understood; clear.

ex am in a tion /eg zam ′ ə nā ′ shən/ *n.* **1.** the act or process of examining. **2.** a test.

ex cel lent /ek ′ sə lənt/ *adj.* very good; outstanding. **—ex cel lent ly**, *adv.*

ex plore /ek splôr ′/ *v.* **1.** to travel in unknown places for the purpose of discovery. **2.** to look through closely; examine.

ex plo sion /ek splō ′ zhən/ *n.* **1.** the act of bursting or expanding suddenly or noisily. **2.** a sudden outburst.

adj.   adjective
adv.   adverb
conj.   conjunction
contr.   contraction
def.   definition
interj.   interjection
n.   noun
pl.   plural
prep.   preposition
pron.   pronoun
sing.   singular
v.   verb
v.i.   intransitive verb
v.t.   transitive verb

...F..............•....

fal con /fôl ′ kən, fal ′ ḳən, fô ′ kən/ *n.* a bird that has pointed wings and a long tail.

fa mil ial /fə mil ′ yəl, fə mil ′ ē əl/ *adj.* of, related to, or like a family.

fa vor/ fā ′ vər/ *n.* **1.** an act of kindness. **2.** friendliness or approval; liking. **3.** a small gift. —*v.* **1.** to show kindness or favor to. **2.** to approve of; believe in; support. **3.** to show special treatment or kindness. **4.** to look like; resemble.

feath er /feth ′ ər/ *n.* one of the light soft body parts that cover a bird's skin. —*v.* to supply, line, or cover with feathers. **—feath er like**, *adv.*

feet /fēt/ *pl., n.* more than one foot.

fence /fens/ *n.* **1.** a structure that is used to surround, protect, or mark off an area. **2.** a person who buys and sells stolen goods. —*v.* **fenced**, **fenc ing**. **1.** to put a fence around. **2.** to fight with a sword or foil; take part in the sport of fencing.

fifth /fifth/ *adj., n.* next after the fourth. —*n.* one of five equal parts; 1/5.

fight /fīt/ *n.* **1.** a struggle between animals, persons, or groups. **2.** a quarrel. **3.** a hard effort to attain a goal. —*v.* **fought**, **fight ing**. **1.** to use weapons or the body to try to hurt or overcome. **2.** to struggle again; try to gain

power over. **3**. to carry on a battle, contest, or struggle.

fire /fīr/ *n*. **1**. the flame, heat, and light given off when wood, paper, or other material burns. **2**. something burning. **3**. a very strong emotion or spirit; passion. *Her eyes were full of fire*. **4**. the shooting of guns. —*v*. **fired**, **fir ing**. **1**. to set on fire; cause to burn. **2**. to dismiss from a job. **3**. to cause to be excited or stirred up. **4**. to set off or be set off; shoot.

fla vor /flā ′ vər/ *n*. **1**. a particular taste. **2**. a special or main quality. —*v*. to give flavor or taste to. —**fla vor ful**, *adj*. —**fla vor some**, *adj*.

flight /flīt/ *n*. **1**. movement through the air with the use of wings; flying. **2**. the distance or course traveled by a bird or aircraft. **3**. a group of things flying through the air together. **4**. a trip in an airplane. **5**. a set of stairs or steps between floors or landings of a building.

flight /flīt/ *n*. the act of running away; escape.

flood light /flud ′ līt ′/ *n*. a lamp that shines brightly over a wide area.

fluff y /fluf ′ ē/ *adj*. **fluff i er, fluff i est**. Covered with or like fluff.

folk /fōk/ *n., pl*. folk or folks. **1**. a people. **2**. family or relatives. —*adj*. coming from or belonging to the common people.

fol low /fol ′ ō/ *v*. **1**. to go or come after, behind, or in back of. **2**. to go along. **3**. to act according to; obey. **4**. to pay attention to and understand. **5**. to make a living from. *Most people along the coast follow the fishing trade*.

foot /fut/ *n., pl*. **feet. 1**. the end part of the leg. **2**. the lowest or supporting part. **3**. the part opposite the head. **4**. a measure of length equal to 12 inches.

force /fôrs/ *n*. **1**. power or strength. **2**. power or strength used against a person or thing. **3**. a group of people who work together. **4**. something that moves a body or stops or changes its motion. **5**. the power to convince or influence. —*v*. **forced**, **forc ing**. **1**. to cause someone to do something against his or her wishes; make. **2**. to cause to open by using force. **3**. to get or make by using power or strength. —**forc er**, *n*.

for eign /fôr ′ ən/ *adj*. **1**. of or from another country. **2**. outside a person's own country. **3**. having to do with other nations or governments. —**for eign ness**, *n*.

for est /fôr ′ ist/ *n*. many trees and plants covering a large area of land; woods.

fought /fôt/ *v*. past tense of *fight*.

foul /foul/ *adj*. **1**. very unpleasant or dirty. **2**. cloudy, rainy, or stormy. **3**. very bad; evil. **4**. breaking the rules; unfair. **5**. outside the foul line in a baseball game. —*n*. **1**. a breaking of rules. **2**. a baseball that is hit outside the foul line. —*v*. **1**. to make dirty. **2**. to tangle or become tangled. **3**. to hit a foul ball in baseball. —**foul ly**, *adv*. —**foul ness**, *n*.

/a/	at
/ā/	ape
/ä/	far
/â/	care
/e/	end
/ē/	me
/i/	it
/ī/	ice
/î/	pierce
/o/	hot
/ō/	old
/ô/	song
/ôr/	fork
/oi/	oil
/ou/	out
/u/	up
/ū/	use
/ü/	rule
/u̇/	pull
/ûr/	turn
/ch/	chin
/ng/	sing
/sh/	shop
/th/	thin
/th/	this
/hw/	white
/zh/	treasure
/ə/	about
	taken
	pencil
	lemon
	circus

frost /frôst/ *n.* **1.** tiny ice crystals that form on a surface when water vapor in the air freezes. **2.** very cold weather during which the temperature is below freezing. —*v.* **1.** to cover with frost. **2.** to cover with frosting or something like frosting.

fruit /früt/ *n., pl.* **fruit** or **fruits**. **1.** the part of the plant that contains the seeds. **2.** a plant part that contains seeds and is fleshy and juicy and good to eat. —**fruit y,** *adj.*

-ful a suffix that means: **1.** having the qualities of; full of. *Fearful* means full of fear. **2.** able to; likely to. *Forgetful* means likely to forget.

fur nace /fûr ′ nis/ *n.* a large, enclosed metal box where heat is produced.

fur nish /fûr ′ nish/ *v.* **1.** to supply with furniture. **2.** to supply or provide. —**fur nish er,** *n.*

adj.	adjective
adv.	adverb
conj.	conjunction
contr.	contraction
def.	definition
interj.	interjection
n.	noun
pl.	plural
prep.	preposition
pron.	pronoun
sing.	singular
v.	verb
v.i.	intransitive verb
v.t.	transitive verb

··**G**··········**G**···

gal lon /gal ′ ən/ *n.* a unit of measure for liquids. A gallon equals four quarts or 3.8 liters.

gar bage /gär ′ bij/ *n.* food and other things that are thrown out.

gar den /gär ′ dən/ *n.* a piece of ground where flowers or vegetables are grown. —*v.* to work in a garden.

gen er al /jen ′ ər əl/ *adj.* **1.** for all; for the whole. **2.** by all or many. **3.** having no limit, restriction, or specialty. **4.** not concerned with details. —*n.* an armed forces officer of the highest rank.

ge og ra phy /jē og ′ rə fē/ *n., pl.* **ge og ra phies.** **1.** the science that deals with the surface of the earth and the plant, animal, and human life on it. **2.** the surface or natural features of a place or region.

ger bil /jûr ′ bəl/ *n.* a small rodent that is native to deserts in Africa and Asia.

glimpse /glimps/ *n.* a quick look; glance. —*v.* **glimpsed, glimps ing.** to see for a moment, glance.

Gla cier Bay /glā ′ sher bā/ *n.* a national park in southeast Alaska.

glo bal /glō ′ bəl/ *adj.* of or relating to the entire world; worldwide.

glo ry /glôr ′ ē/ *n., pl.* **glo ries. 1.** great praise; honor; fame. **2.** great beauty; splendor; magnificence. *The sun shone in all its glory.* —**glor i ous,** *adj.*

glos sa ry /glos ′ ə rē/ *n., pl.* **glos sa ries.** an alphabetical list of difficult words and their meanings.

glove /gluv/ *n.* a covering for the hand.

gnarled /närld/ *adj.* having a rough, twisted, or rugged look.

gnaw /nô/ **gnawed, gnawed** or **gnawn, gnaw ing**. *v.* to bite again and again in order to wear away little by little.

goose /güs/ *n., pl.* **geese**. 1. a bird that looks like a duck but is larger and has a longer neck. 2. a female bird of this kind.

gov ern /guv ′ ərn/ *v.* to rule, control, or manage. —**gov ern able**, *adj.*

grand /grand/ *adj.* 1. large and splendid. 2. including everything; complete. 3. most important; main. 4. very good or excellent.

Grand Can yon /grand kan ′ yen/ *n.* a national park in northern Arizona.

Grand Te ton /grand tē ′ tən/ *n.* a national park in west central Wyoming.

grand stand /grand ′ stand ′/ *n.* the main place where people sit when watching a parade or sports event.

grate /grāt/ *v.* to make into small pieces or shreds by rubbing against a rough surface.

grav i ty /grav ′ i tē/ *n., pl.* **grav i ties**. 1. the force that pulls things toward the center of the earth. 2. serious nature. *Because of the gravity of the situation, troops were sent in.*

grease /*n.* grēs; *v.* grēs, grēz/ *n.* 1. melted animal fat. 2. a very thick, oily material. —*v.* **greased, greas ing**. to rub or put grease on or in.

great /grāt/ *adj.* 1. very large in size, number, or amount. 2. very important, excellent, or remarkable. 3. more than is usual; much.

greed y /grē ′ dē/ *adj.* **greed i er, greed i est**. having a great and selfish desire for more than one's share of something.

growl /groul/ *v.* to make a deep, harsh, rumbling sound in the throat. —*n.* a deep, harsh, rumbling sound made in the throat.

growth /grōth/ *n.* 1. the process of growing. 2. something that has grown.

grum ble /grum ′ bəl/ *v.* **grum bled, grum bling**. 1. to complain in a low voice. 2. to make a low rumbling sound. —*n.* 1. unhappy complaining or muttering. 2. a low, rumbling sound. —**grum bler**, *n.*

guest /gest/ *n.* 1. a person who visits another's house. 2. a customer in a restaurant, hotel, or similar place.

guilt /gilt/ *n.* 1. the condition or fact of having done something wrong or having broken the law. 2. a feeling of having done something wrong; shame. —**guilt less**, *adj.*

gym nast /jim ′ nast, jim ′ nəst/ *n.* a person skilled in gymnastics or competing in gymnastics.

/a/	at
/ā/	ape
/ä/	far
/â/	care
/e/	end
/ē/	me
/i/	it
/ī/	ice
/î/	pierce
/o/	hot
/ō/	old
/ô/	song
/ôr/	fork
/oi/	oil
/ou/	out
/u/	up
/ū/	use
/ü/	rule
/u̇/	pull
/ûr/	turn
/ch/	chin
/ng/	sing
/sh/	shop
/th/	thin
/th/	this
/hw/	white
/zh/	treasure
/ə/	about
	taken
	pencil
	lemon
	circus

half back /haf ′bak ′/ *n.* a football player who runs with the ball, catches or throws passes, or blocks.

han di cap /han ′ dē kap ′/ *n.* **1.** anything that makes it harder for a person to do well or get ahead. **2.** an advantage given to a weaker player or team or a disadvantage given to a stronger player or team at the start of a game. —*v.* **hand i capped, hand i cap ping. 1.** to place at a disadvantage; hamper. **2.** (in a contest) to give one or more handicaps to.

han dle /han ′ dəl/ *n.* the part of an object that is made to be grasped by the hand. —*v.* **han dled, han dling. 1.** to touch or hold with the hand. **2.** to manage, control, or deal with. —**han dler,** *n.*

hand shake /hand ′ shāk ′/ *n.* an act in which two people grip and shake each other's hand.

hand some /han ′ səm/ *adj.* **1.** having a pleasing appearance. **2.** fairly large or generous. —**hand some ly,** *adv.* —**hand some ness,** *n.*

hang ing /hang ′ ing/ —*v.* **1.** attached to something above. **2.** leaning over; overhanging. **3.** placed on a steep slope.

hap pen /hap ′ ən/ *v.* **1.** to take place; occur. **2.** to come or go by chance. **3.** to be done.

adj.	adjective
adv.	adverb
conj.	conjunction
contr.	contraction
def.	definition
interj.	interjection
n.	noun
pl.	plural
prep.	preposition
pron.	pronoun
sing.	singular
v.	verb
v.i.	intransitive verb
v.t.	transitive verb

harm ful /härm ′ fəl/ *adj.* causing harm; damaging. —**harm ful ly,** *adv.* —**harm ful ness,** *n.*

has ten /hā ′ sən/ *v.* **1.** to move quickly; hurry. **2.** to make something happen faster; speed up.

has ty /hās ′ tē/ *adj.* **hast i er, hast i est. 1.** quick; hurried. **2.** too quick; careless or reckless. —**hast i ly,** *adv.* —**hast i ness,** *n.*

Ha wai i Vol ca noes /hə wī ′ ē vol kā ′ nōz/ *n.* a national park on the island of Hawaii.

head /hed/ *n.* **1.** the top part of the human body. **2.** the top or front part of any other animal that is like a human head. **3.** the top or front part of something. **4.** a firm, rounded cluster of leaves or flowers. **5.** a person who is above others in rank; chief. —*adj.* **1.** top, chief, or front. —*v.* to be or go to the top or front of, lead. **2.** to be in charge of. **3.** to direct or move in a direction.

health /helth/ *n.* **1.** the condition of being well and without disease or injury. **2.** the condition of the body or mind.

heart /härt/ *n.* **1.** the hollow organ in the body that pumps blood through the arteries and veins. **2.** the center of a person's feelings. **3.** spirit; courage. **4.** the center or middle of anything. **5.** a playing card marked with one or more red figures like this: ♥. **6.** anything shaped like a heart.

heav y /hev ′ ē/ *adj.* **heav i er, heav i est.**
1. having great weight; hard to lift or
move. **2.** having more than the usual
weight. **3.** large in size or amount.
4. hard to do, carry out, or bear.
—**heav i ly,** *adv.* —**heav i ness,** *n.*

hel i cop ter /hel ′ i kop ′ ter/ *n.* an
aircraft that is kept in the air by
blades that rotate above the craft.

he ro /hîr ′ ō/ *n., pl.* **he roes. 1.** a person who is looked up to by others
because of his or her great achieve-
ments or fine qualities. **2.** the main
male character in a play, story, or
poem. **3.** a big sandwich on a long
roll with a thick crust.

hoarse /hôrs/ *adj.* **hoars er, hoars est.**
1. having a rough or harsh, deep
sound. **2.** having a harsh voice.
—**hoarse ly,** *adv.* —**hoarse ness,** *n.*

hock ey /hok ′ ē/ *n.* **1.** a game played
on ice by two teams of six players
each. The players wear ice skates and
hit a rubber disk, called a puck, with
curved sticks. Each team tries to get
the puck into the other team's goal.
2. a game played on a field by two
teams of eleven players each. Curved
sticks are used to hit a ball along the
ground into the other team's goal.

hon est /on ′ ist/ *adj.* **1.** truthful, fair, or
trustworthy. **2.** earned or gotten fair-
ly. —**hon est ly,** *adv.* —**hon est ness,** *n.*

hon ey /hun ′ ē/ *n.* **1.** a thick, sweet
liquid made by bees. **2.** a very dear
person or thing.

hon or /on ′ ər/ *n.* **1.** a sense of what
is right or honest; high moral stan-
dards. **2.** a good name or reputation.
3. something given or done to show
great respect or appreciation.
4. Honor. a title of respect used in
speaking to or of a judge, mayor, or
other official. "*Your Honor.*" —*v.* to
show or feel great respect for a person or thing.

horse /hôrs/ *n.* **1.** a large animal with
four legs, hooves, and a long, flowing
mane. **2.** any mammal belonging to
the horse family that includes horses,
zebras, and asses. **3.** a frame with legs,
used to hold things like wood being
sawed. **4.** a heavy leather pad on supporting legs, used in gymnastics for
doing certain exercises.

ho tel /hō tel ′/ *n.* a building with
many rooms that people pay to sleep
in.

hour /our/ *n.* **1.** a unit of time equal
to sixty minutes. **2.** a time of the day
that is shown on a clock or watch.
3. the time for anything.

how ev er /hou ev ′ ər/ *conj.* in spite
of that; yet. —*adv.* **1.** in whatever way.
2. to whatever degree.

hun ger /hung ′ gər/ *n.* **1.** pain or
weakness caused by not eating
enough food. **2.** the feeling of
wanting or needing food. **3.** a
strong wish or need for something. —*v.* to have a strong wish or
need for something. —**hun gri ly,**
adv. —**hun gri ness,** *n.*

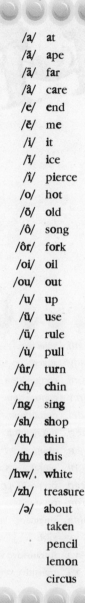

/a/	at
/ā/	ape
/ä/	far
/â/	care
/e/	end
/ē/	me
/i/	it
/ī/	ice
/î/	pierce
/o/	hot
/ō/	old
/ô/	song
/ôr/	fork
/oi/	oil
/ou/	out
/u/	up
/ū/	use
/ü/	rule
/ù/	pull
/ûr/	turn
/ch/	chin
/ng/	sing
/sh/	shop
/th/	thin
/th/	this
/hw/	white
/zh/	treasure
/ə/	about
	taken
	pencil
	lemon
	circus

hur dle /hûr ′ dəl/ *n.* **1.** a barrier that has to be jumped over in a race. **2.** a difficulty or problem. —*v.* **hur dled, hur dling.** to jump over while running. —**hur dler,** *n.*

-ic a suffix that means having the qualities of; being or like. *Angelic* means like an angel.

i de a /ī dē ′ ə/ *n.* **1.** a picture or thought formed in the mind. **2.** a belief; opinion. **3.** the purpose. **4.** the main meaning; point.

ig loo /ig ′ lü/ *n.* a hut shaped like a dome that is used by the Inuit to live in.

im- a prefix that means not or a lack of. *Impatience* means a lack of patience.

im i tate /im ′ i tāt/ *v.* **im i tat ed, im i tat ing.** **1.** to try to act just like another person. **2.** to look like; resemble.

im mi grant /im ′ i grənt/ *n.* a person who comes to live in a country in which he or she was not born.

im por tant /im pôr ′ tənt/ *adj.* **1.** having great value or meaning. **2.** having a high position or much power. —**im por tant ly,** *adv.*

in- a prefix that means **1.** not. *Inappropriate* means not appropriate. **2.** in or into. *Intake* means the amount of something taken in.

inch /inch/ *n., pl.* **inch es.** a measure of length that equals 1/12 of a foot. One inch is the same as 2.54 centimeters. —*v.* to move very slowly.

in dig nant /in dig ′ nənt/ *adj.* filled with anger about something unfair, wrong, or bad. —**in dig nant ly,** *adv.*

in stinct /in ′ stingkt ′/ *n.* a way of acting or behaving that a person or animal is born with and does not have to learn.

is land /ī ′ lənd/ *n.* **1.** a body of land that is completely surrounded by water. **2.** something that looks like an island.

is n't /iz ′ ənt/ *contr.* shortened form of "is not."

-ist a suffix that means one who does or makes something. A *tourist* is a person who tours.

-itis a suffix that means inflammation of. *Tonsillitis* means inflammation of the tonsils.

-ity a suffix that means the state, conditon, or quality of being. *Reality* means the quality of being real.

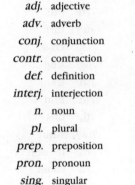

adj.	adjective
adv.	adverb
conj.	conjunction
contr.	contraction
def.	definition
interj.	interjection
n.	noun
pl.	plural
prep.	preposition
pron.	pronoun
sing.	singular
v.	verb
v.i.	intransitive verb
v.t.	transitive verb

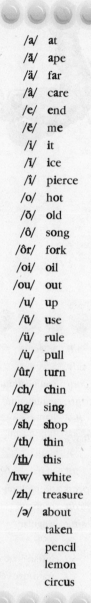

...J......................K...............

jazz /jaz/ *n.* music that has strong rhythm and accented notes that fall in unexpected places.

joint /joint/ *n.* **1.** the place or part where two or more bones meet or come together. **2.** the part or space between two joints. **3.** the place or part where any two or more things meet or come together. —*adj.* belonging to or done by two or more people.

jour nal /jûr ′ nəl/ *n.* **1.** a regular record or account. **2.** a magazine or newspaper.

jour ney /jûr ′ nē/ *n.* a long trip. —*v.* to make a trip; travel.

juice /jüs/ *n.* **1.** the liquid from vegetables, fruits, or meats. **2.** a fluid produced inside the body.

jun ior /jün ′ yər/ *adj.* **1.** the younger of two. **2.** of or for younger people. **3.** the year before the last year in high school or college. **4.** having a lower position or rank. —*n.* a person who is younger than another.

jus tice /jus ′ tis/ *n.* **1.** fair or right treatment or action. **2.** the quality or condition of being fair and right. **3.** a judge of the Supreme Court of the United States.

ken nel /ken ′ əl/ *n.* **1.** a building where dogs are kept. **2.** a place where dogs are raised and trained or cared for while the owner is away.

kid ney /kid ′ nē/ *n.* **1.** either of two organs in the body that are shaped like a very large bean. **2.** the kidneys of certain animals when used as food.

ki lom e ter /ki lom ′ i tər, kil ′ ə mē ′ tər/ *n.* a unit of length in the metric system. A kilometer is equal to 1,000 meters, or about 0.62 of a mile.

kind [1] /kīnd/ *adj.* gentle, generous, and friendly.

kind [2] /kīnd/ *n.* **1.** a group of things that are the same in some way. **2.** one of a group of people or things that are different or special in some way. *That's not the kind of saw that can cut a metal pipe.*

kneel /nēl/ *v.* **knelt** or **kneeled**, **kneel ing.** to go down on a bent knee or knees. —**kneel er**, n.

knot /not/ *n.* **1.** the place where pieces of thread, string, or cord are tied around each other. **2.** a tangle or lump. **3.** a small group of people or things. **4.** a dark, hard, round spot in a board. **5.** a measurement of speed used on ships, boats, and aircraft. —*v.* **knot ted, knot ting.** to tie or tangle in or with a knot or knots.

/a/	at
/ā/	ape
/ä/	far
/â/	care
/e/	end
/ē/	me
/i/	it
/ī/	ice
/î/	pierce
/o/	hot
/ō/	old
/ô/	song
/ôr/	fork
/oi/	oil
/ou/	out
/u/	up
/ū/	use
/ü/	rule
/ù/	pull
/ûr/	turn
/ch/	chin
/ng/	sing
/sh/	shop
/th/	thin
/th/	this
/hw/	white
/zh/	treasure
/ə/	about
	taken
	pencil
	lemon
	circus

159

la bel /lā ′ bəl/ *n.* a piece of cloth or other material that is fastened to something and gives information about it. —*v.* **1.** to put a label on. **2.** to describe as, using a word or short phrase. *The teacher labeled the picnic a success.*

lad der /lad ′ ər/ *n.* a device used for climbing.

lad y /lā ′ dē/ *n., pl.* **lad ies. 1.** any woman. **2.** a girl or woman who is polite or has good manners. **3.** a woman who has a high social position.

adj.	adjective
adv.	adverb
conj.	conjunction
contr.	contraction
def.	definition
interj.	interjection
n.	noun
pl.	plural
prep.	preposition
pron.	pronoun
sing.	singular
v.	verb
v.i.	intransitive verb
v.t.	transitive verb

lamb /lam/ *n.* **1.** a young sheep. **2.** the meat from a lamb.

lan tern /lan ′ tərn/ *n.* a covering or container for a light.

la ser /lā ′ zər/ *n.* a device that makes a very narrow but strong beam of light.

laugh /laf/ *v.* to make sounds that show amusement, happiness, or ridicule. —*n.* the act or sound of laughing. **—laugh ter**, *n.*

league [1] /lēg/ *n.* a number of people, groups, or countries joined together for a common purpose.

league [2] /lēg/ *n.* a measure of distance that was used in the past. A league is equal to about three miles.

leath er /leth ′ ər/ *n.* a material made from an animal skin that has been cleaned and tanned.

les son /les ′ ən/ *n.* **1.** something to be learned, taught, or studied. **2.** a period of time given to instruction.

lev el /lev ′ əl/ *adj.* **1.** having a flat, horizontal surface; even. **2.** at the same height or position. —*n.* height. **3.** a position or rank in a process, series, or order. **4.** a floor or story of a structure. **5.** a tool. —*v.* **1.** to make flat. **2.** to bring to the level of the ground; destroy. **—lev el er**, *n.* **—lev el ly**, *adv.* **—lev el ness**, *n.*

life boat /līf ′ bot ′/ *n.* a boat used for saving lives at sea or along the shore.

lig a ment /lig ′ ə mənt/ *n.* a band of strong tissue.

light ning /līt ′ ning/ *n.* a flash of light in the sky.

like [1] /līk/ *prep.* **1.** almost the same as; similar to. **2.** such as. **3.** having the desire to. **4.** giving a promise or indication of. —*adj.* similar or equal. —*conj.* **1.** in a way that; as. *This soup doesn't taste like it has enough salt.* **2.** as if; as though.

like [2] /līk/ *v.* **liked, lik ing.** to be fond of; enjoy.

lim it /lim ′ it/ *n.* the point at which something ends or must end. —*v.* to keep within a bound or bounds; restrict.

lim i ta tion /lim ′ i tā ′ shən/ *n.* something that limits.

lis ten /lis ′ ən/ *v.* to try to hear; pay attention in order to hear. —**lis ten er**, *n.*

li ter /lē ′ tər/ *n.* a unit of measurement in the metric system. A liter is a little larger than a quart of liquid.

lo cal / lō ′ kəl/ *adj.* **1.** having to do with a particular place. **2.** stopping at all or most of the stops along a route; not an express. **3.** having to do with or affecting only a part of the body. *a local anesthetic.* —*n.* a train, bus, or subway that stops at most or all of the stops along its route. —**lo cal ly**, *adv.*

lo ca tion /lō kā ′ shən/ *n.* **1.** the place where something is located; site. **2.** the act of locating.

lose /lüz/ *v.* **lost, los ing. 1.** to have no longer; be without. **2.** to fail to keep. **3.** to fail to win. **4.** to fail to use; waste.

love ly /luv ′ lē/ *adj.* **love li er, love li est. 1.** having a beautiful appearance or a warm character. **2.** enjoyable.

lu nar /lü ′ nər/ *adj.* of or having to do with the moon.

lung /lung/ *n.* one of the two organs for breathing in the chest of human beings and other animals with backbones.

-ly a suffix that means in a certain way or manner. *Perfectly* means in a perfect way.

-ly a suffix that means *like. Friendly* means like a friend.

• • • M • • • • • • • • • • • • • •

ma chine /mə shēn ′/ *n.* **1.** a device that does some particular job. **2.** a simple device that lessens the force needed to move an object.

mag net /mag ′ nit/ *n.* a piece of stone, metal, or other material that can attract iron or steel.

main tain /mān tān ′/ *v.* **1.** to continue to have to do; go on with; keep. **2.** to take care of. **3.** to say in a firm and sure way.

male /māl/ *adj.* **1.** of or having to do with men or boys. **2.** having to do with or belonging to the sex that can fertilize female eggs.

mam mal /mam ′ əl/ *n.* the kind of animal that is warm-blooded and has a backbone.

Mam moth Cave /mam ′ əth cāv/ *n.* a national park in central Kentucky.

/a/	at
/ā/	ape
/ä/	far
/â/	care
/e/	end
/ē/	me
/i/	it
/ī/	ice
/î/	pierce
/o/	hot
/ō/	old
/ô/	song
/ôr/	fork
/oi/	oil
/ou/	out
/u/	up
/ū/	use
/ü/	rule
/ů/	pull
/ûr/	turn
/ch/	chin
/ng/	sing
/sh/	shop
/th/	thin
/th/	this
/hw/	white
/zh/	treasure
/ə/	about
	taken
	pencil
	lemon
	circus

mar ble /mär ′ bəl/ *n.* **1.** a type of hard, smooth stone. **2.** a small, hard ball of glass used in games.

mar ket /mär ′ kit/ *n.* **1.** a place or store where food or goods are for sale. **2.** a demand for something that is for sale. —*v.* to buy or sell goods at a market.

mar row /mar ′ ō/ *n.* the soft substance that fills the hollow parts of bones.

mar vel /mär ′ vel/ *n.* a wonderful or astonishing thing. —*v.* to feel wonder and astonishment.

adj.	adjective
adv.	adverb
conj.	conjunction
contr.	contraction
def.	definition
interj.	interjection
n.	noun
pl.	plural
prep.	preposition
pron.	pronoun
sing.	singular
v.	verb
v.i.	intransitive verb
v.t.	transitive verb

mean /mēn/ *v.* **meant, mean ing. 1.** to have in mind; want to do or say. **2.** to have as a purpose; intend. **3.** to be defined as; have a particular purpose.

meant /ment/ *v.* past tense and past participle of *mean.*

meas ure /mezh ′ ər/ *v.* **1.** to find or show the size, weight, or amount of something. **2.** to mark off or set apart by measuring. —*n.* **1.** the size, weight, or amount of something. **2.** a unit, standard, or system of measurement.

med dle /med ′ əl/ *v.* **med dled, med dling.** to take part in another person's business without being asked or wanted; interfere.

med i cine /med ′ ə sin/ *n.* **1.** a drug or other substance used to prevent or cure disease or to relieve pain. **2.** the science or practice of detecting, treating, or preventing disease or injury.

-ment a suffix that means the state of being. *Amazement* means a state of being amazed.

met al /met ′ əl/ *n.* a substance that usually has a shiny surface, can be melted, and can conduct heat and electricity.

me ter /mē ′ tər/ *n.* **1.** the basic unit of length in the metric system. A meter is equal to 39.37 inches, or slightly more than 3 1/4 feet. **2.** the basic pattern of rhythm that accented notes or beats give to a piece of music.

micro- a prefix that means very small. A *microscope* is a scope for very small objects.

mi cro chip /mī ′ krə chip/ *n.* a small, thin slice of special material that usually contains a large number of tiny electronic parts.

mi cro scope /mī ′ krə skōp ′/ *n.* a device that is used to look at things that are too small to be seen with the naked eye.

mid dle /mid ′ əl/ *adj.* halfway between two things, sides, times, or the like. —*n.* something that is halfway between two things, sides, times, or the like.

might /mīt/ *n.* power or strength. —**might y,** *adj.*

mile /mīl/ *n.* a measure of distance equal to 5,280 feet.

mil li me ter /mil ′ ə mē tər/ *n.* a unit of length in the metric system. A millimeter is equal to one thousandth of a meter, or about .039 of an inch.

min ute /min ′ it/ *n., pl.* **1.** a unit of time equal to sixty seconds. **2.** a moment in time; instant. **3. min utes** a written report of what was said and done at a meeting.

mis- a prefix that means: **1.** bad; wrong. *Misfortune* means bad fortune. **2.** in a bad or wrong way. *Misprounounce* means to pronounce in the wrong way.

mis chief /mis ′ chif/ *n.* an action or conduct that may seem playful but that causes harm or trouble.

mis for tune /mis fôr ′ chən/ *n.* **1.** bad luck. **2.** an unlucky event or happening.

mis judge /mis juj ′/ *v.* to judge incorrectly or unfairly.

mis lay /mis lā ′/ *v.* **mis laid, mis lay ing.** to put in a place that is later forgotten.

mis lead /mis lēd ′/ *v.* **mis led, mis lead ing. 1.** to lead or guide in the wrong direction. **2.** to lead into a mistaken or wrong thought or action.

mis match /mis mach ′/ *v.* to match or join together unwisely. —*n.* an unwise or unsuitable match.

mis print /mis ′ print ′, mis print ′/ *n.* an error in printing. —*v.* to print incorrectly.

mis pro nounce /mis ′ prə nouns ′/ *v.* to pronounce a word or sound in the wrong way.

mis sile /mis ′ əl/ *n.* **1.** anything that is thrown or shot through the air. **2.** a rocket that is used to launch a space capsule, satellite, or weapon.

mis sion /mish ′ ən/ *n.* **1.** a group of people who are sent somewhere to do a special job. **2.** a special job or task. **3.** a church or other place where a group of missionaries work.

mis spell /mis spel ′/ *v.* **mis spelled** or **mis spelt** /mis spelt/, **mis spell ing.** to spell a word incorrectly.

mis treat /mis trēt ′/ *v.* to be cruel, rough, or unkind to; treat badly.

mis un der stand /mis ′ un dər stand ′/ *v.* **mis un der stood, mis un der stand ing.** to understand someone or something incorrectly.

mod el /mod ′ əl/ *n.* **1.** a copy of something. **2.** a style or type of thing. —*adj.* worthy of being imitated. —*v.* **1.** to make or design something. **2.** to follow or copy someone or something.

mod ern /mod ′ ərn/ *adj.* having to do with the present or recent time.

mon ey /mun ′ ē/ *n.* the coins and paper currency of a country.

/a/	at
/ā/	ape
/ä/	far
/â/	care
/e/	end
/ē/	me
/i/	it
/ī/	ice
/î/	pierce
/o/	hot
/ō/	old
/ô/	song
/ôr/	fork
/oi/	oil
/ou/	out
/u/	up
/ū/	use
/ü/	rule
/u̇/	pull
/ûr/	turn
/ch/	chin
/ng/	sing
/sh/	shop
/th/	thin
/th/	this
/hw/	white
/zh/	treasure
/ə/	about
	taken
	pencil
	lemon
	circus

moose /müs/ *n., pl.* **moose**. a large, heavy animal related to the deer that lives in forests in cold northern regions of North America.

mor tal /môr ′ təl/ *adj.* **1**. certain to die. **2**. causing death. **3**. very great; intense. **4**. very hostile. —*n.* a person, human being.

mos qui to /mə skē ′ tō/ *n., pl.* **mos qui toes** or **mos qui tos**. a small insect with two wings.

mo tion /mō ′ shən/ *n.* **1**. the act of changing place or position; movement. **2**. a formal suggestion made at a meeting. —*v.* to move the hand or another part of the body as a sign of something.

adj.	adjective
adv.	adverb
conj.	conjunction
contr.	contraction
def.	definition
interj.	interjection
n.	noun
pl.	plural
prep.	preposition
pron.	pronoun
sing.	singular
v.	verb
v.i.	intransitive verb
v.t.	transitive verb

mo tor /mō ′ tər/ *n.* a machine that provides motion or power to make things run or work. —*adj.* **1**. having to do with a motor or something run by a motor. **2**. having to do with the nerves of a person's body that control motion. —*v.* to travel by car.

mo tor cy cle /mō ′ tər sī ′ kəl/ *n.* a vehicle with two wheels that is bigger and heavier than a bicycle and is powered by an engine.

Mount Rain ier /mount rā ′ nir *or* rā nir ′/ *n.* a national park near Seattle, Washington.

moun tain /moun ′ tən/ *n.* **1**. a mass of land that rises very high above the surrounding area. **2**. a very large pile or amount of something.

mus cle /mus ′ əl/ *n.* a tissue in the body that is made of strong fibers.

mu se um /mū zē ′ əm/ *n.* a building where objects of art, science, or history are displayed.

mus ic /mū ′ zik/ *n.* **1**. a pleasing combination of sounds. **2**. a musical composition.

mus sel /mus ′ əl/ *n.* an animal that looks like a clam.

mys ter y /mis ′ tə rē/ *n., pl.* **my ster ies**. **1**. something that cannot be known, explained, or understood. **2**. a book, play, or other story about a crime that is puzzling. —**mys te ri ous**, *adj.*

myth /mith/ *n.* **1**. a story that tells about a belief of a group of people. **2**. a person or thing that is not real or true.

• • • N • • • • • • • • • • • • • • •

nat u ral /nach ′ ər əl/ *adj.* found in nature; not made by people; not artificial.

nec es sar y /nes ′ ə ser ′ ē/ *adj.* **1**. that must be had or done; required. **2**. that cannot be avoided; certain. —*n.* **nec es sar ies**. something that cannot be done without.

nee dle /nē ′ dəl/ *n.* **1**. a thin, pointed instrument with a hole at one end.

2. a pointer on a compass or dial. **3.** a sharp, thin, hollow tube that is used to put fluid into or remove fluid from the body. **4.** a thin rod used for knitting. **5.** the thin, pointed leaves on a fir or pine tree. —*v.* **nee dled**; **nee dling**. to tease or annoy.

nee dle point /nē ′ dəl point ′/ *n.* embroidery done on a cloth.

neph ew /nef ′ ū/ *n.* **1.** the son of one's brother or sister. **2.** the son of one's brother-in-law or sister-in-law.

nerve /nûrv/ *n.* **1.** a bundle of fibers that carries messages between the brain and the spinal cord and other parts of the body. **2.** courage or bravery.

news pa per /nüz ′ pā ′ pər, nūz ′ pā ′ pər/ *n.* a publication that contains news, opinions on local and national happenings, and advertisements.

non- a prefix that means not or the opposite of. *Nonfiction* means not fiction.

none /nun/ *pron.* **1.** no one; not one. **2.** no part; not any. —*adv.* not at all.

noo dle /nü ′ dəl/ *n.* a flat strip of dried dough.

nor mal /nôr ′ məl/ *adj.* **1.** conforming to a standard, pattern, or model. **2.** having average mental or physical development. —*n.* the usual or regular condition or level.

noth ing /nuth ′ ing/ *n.* **1.** no thing; not anything. **2.** a person or thing that is of no importance. **3.** zero. —*adv.* in no way; not at all.

nui sance /nü ′ səns, nū ′ səns/ *n.* a person, thing, or action that annoys or offends.

o bey /ō bā ′/ *v.* **1.** to carry out the orders, wishes, or instructions of. **2.** to carry out or follow.

ob ser va tion /ob zer vā ′ shən/ *n.* **1.** the act or power of noticing. **2.** the condition of being seen. **3.** something said; comment. —**ob ser va tion al**, *adj.*

oc cur /ə kûr ′/ *v.* **oc curred, oc cur ring. 1.** to take place; happen. **2.** to be found; appear. **3.** to come into one's thought; suggest itself.

oc to pus /ok ′ tə pəs/ *n., pl.* **oc to pus es** or **oc to pi.** an animal that lives in salt water and has a soft, rounded body and eight arms.

of fer /ô ′ fer/ *v.* **of fered, of fer ring. 1.** to present for acceptance or refusal. **2.** to present as an act of religious worship or devotion.

of fi cer /ô ′ fə sər/ *n.* a person who has a position of authority, trust, or responsibility.

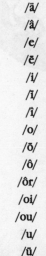

/a/	at
/ā/	ape
/ä/	far
/â/	care
/e/	end
/ē/	me
/i/	it
/ī/	ice
/î/	pierce
/o/	hot
/ō/	old
/ô/	song
/ôr/	fork
/oi/	oil
/ou/	out
/u/	up
/ū/	use
/ü/	rule
/ù/	pull
/ûr/	turn
/ch/	chin
/ng/	sing
/sh/	shop
/th/	thin
/th/	this
/hw/	white
/zh/	treasure
/ə/	about
	taken
	pencil
	lemon
	circus

adj.	adjective
adv.	adverb
conj.	conjunction
contr.	contraction
def.	definition
interj.	interjection
n.	noun
pl.	plural
prep.	preposition
pron.	pronoun
sing.	singular
v.	verb
v.i.	intransitive verb
v.t.	transitive verb

of ten /ô ′ fən/ *adv.* many times; frequently.

on ion /un ′ yen/ *n.* the round or oval bulb of a plant that is also known as an onion. —**on ion like**, *adj.*

op er a tor /op ′ ə rā ′ tər/ *n.* a person who operates a machine or other device.

or bit /ôr ′ bit/ *n.* **1.** the path that a planet or other heavenly body follows as it moves in a circle around another heavenly body. **2.** one complete trip of a spacecraft along such a path. —*v.* to move in an orbit around a heavenly body.

or der /ôr ′ dər/ *n.* **1.** a command to do something. **2.** the way in which things are arranged. **3.** a condition in which laws or rules are obeyed. **4.** clean, neat, or proper position. **5.** a request for goods. **6.** goods that have been requested or supplied. **7.** a group of people who live under the same rules or belong to the same organization. **8.** a related group of animals, plants, or other living things. —*v.* **1.** give an order to; command. **2.** to place an order for; ask for. **3.** to put into proper order.

or gan /ôr ′ gən/ *n.* **1.** a musical instrument. **2.** a part of an animal or plant that is made up of several kinds of tissues.

or phan /ôr ′ fən/ *n.* a child whose parents are dead. —*v.* to make an orphan of. *The war orphaned hundreds of children.*

ought /ôt/ *v.* auxiliary verb that is used in the following ways: **1.** to express an obligation. **2.** to express what is likely. **3.** to offer advice.

ounce /ouns/ *n.* **1.** a unit of weight equal to 1/16 of a pound. Sixteen ounces equal one pound. **2.** a unit of measure for liquids. Thirty-two ounces equal one quart. **3.** a small bit.

-ous a suffix that means having or full of. *Dangerous* means full of danger.

out line /out ′ līn ′/ *n.* **1.** the shape of an object formed by following along its outer edge. **2.** a summary of a story, speech, or other writing. —*v.* **out lined**, **out lin ing**. **1.** to give a summary of. **2.** to draw the outline of.

out ward /out ′ wərd/ *adv.* to or toward the outside. —*adj.* **1.** toward or on the outside. **2.** capable of being seen from the outside. Also (*adv.*) **out wards** /out ′ werdz/ —**out ward ness**, *n.*

o ver grow /ō ′ vər grō ′/ *v.* **o ver grew**, **o ver grown**, **o ver grow ing**. to grow over.

own /ōn/ *adj.* of, having to do with, or belonging to oneself or itself. —*n.* something that belongs to one. —*v.* **1.** to have as belonging to one. **2.** to admit doing something.

own er /ō ′ nər/ *n.* a person who owns something.

own er ship /ō ′ nər ship ′/ *n.* the state of possessing something.

ox y gen /ok ′ sə jən/ *n.* a gas that has no color or smell.

· · · P · · · · · · · · · · · · · P · · ·

pad dle /pad ′ əl/ *n.* **1.** a short oar with a wide, flat blade. **2.** a small, broad board with a short handle. **3.** a flat, wooden tool. —*v.* **pad dled, pad dling. 1.** to move a canoe or other boat with a paddle. **2.** to hit with a paddle or with the hand, spank. —**pad dle like**, *adj.* —**pad dler**, *n.*

pal ace /pal ′ is/ *n.* a very large, grand building where a king, queen, or other ruler lives.

par a graph /par ′ ə graf ′/ *n.* a part of something written, made up of one or more sentences about a particular subject or idea. —**par a graph er**, *n.*

par cel /pär ′ səl/ *n.* **1.** something wrapped up. **2.** a piece or section. —*v.* to divide into sections.

par ent /pâr ′ ənt/ *n.* **1.** a father or mother. **2.** a living thing, such as an animal or plant, that has produced offspring.

par ka /pär ′ kə/ *n.* a warm fur or cloth jacket with a hood.

par rot /par ′ ət/ *n.* a bird with a wide, curved bill, a long, pointed tail, and glossy, brightly colored feathers. —**par rot like**, *adj.*

pay /pā/ *v.* **paid, pay ing. 1.** to give money to someone in return for things or work. **2.** to give money in order to settle. **3.** to be worthwhile or good for someone. **4.** to give or suffer something in return. **5.** to make or give. —*n.* money given in return for things or work.

peace /pēs/ *n.* **1.** freedom from fighting or conflict. **2.** a lack of noise or disorder. **3.** public order or safety.

ped al /ped ′ əl/ *n.* a lever or other device that is moved by the foot to run or control something. —*v.* to work or use the pedals of something.

ped dle /ped ′ əl/ *v.* **ped dled, ped dling.** to carry goods from place to place and offer them for sale.

pel i can /pel ′ i kən/ *n.* a large bird that lives near the water and has a pouch under its long bill.

pen nant /pən ′ ənt/ *n.* a long, narrow flag that is shaped like a triangle.

pe ri od /pîr ′ ē əd/ *n.* **1.** a portion of time. **2.** a punctuation mark (.).

per ma nent /pûr ′ mə nənt/ *adj.* lasting or meant to last; enduring. —**per ma nent ly**, *adv.*

/a/	at
/ā/	ape
/ä/	far
/â/	care
/e/	end
/ē/	me
/i/	it
/ī/	ice
/î/	pierce
/o/	hot
/ō/	old
/ô/	song
/ôr/	fork
/oi/	oil
/ou/	out
/u/	up
/ū/	use
/ü/	rule
/ù/	pull
/ûr/	turn
/ch/	chin
/ng/	sing
/sh/	shop
/th/	thin
/th/	this
/hw/	white
/zh/	treasure
/ə/	about
	taken
	pencil
	lemon
	circus

per son /pûr ′ sən/ *n*. **1**. a man, woman, or child; person. **2**. the body of and clothing worn by a human being. **3**. any of three groups of personal pronouns and verb forms.

pet al /pet ′ əl/ *n*. one of the parts of a flower. **—pet aled**; also, **pet alled**, *adj*. **—pet al like**, *adj*.

Pet ri fied For est /pet ′ rə fīd ′ fôr ′ ist/ *n*. a national park in eastern Arizona.

phan tom /fan ′ təm/ *n*. something that appears to be real but is not.

phar ma cy /fär ′ mə sē/ *n*., *pl*. **phar ma cies**. a store where drugs and medicine are sold; drugstore.

pho to graph /fō ′ tə graf/ *n*. a picture that is made by using a camera. **—***v*. to take a picture with a camera.

pi a no /pē an ′ ō, pyan ′ ō/ *n*. a musical instrument.

pick /pik/ *v*. **1**. to take from a number offered. **2**. to gather with the fingers. **3**. to remove with the fingers or something pointed. **4**. to pull at and let go. **5**. to cause on purpose. **6**. to steal the contents of. **7**. to open with a wire or something pointed. **8**. to eat in small amounts. **—***n*. **1**. the best one or ones. **2**. an act of choosing. **3**. a small, thin piece of plastic or other material. **—pick er**, *n*.

pick /pik/ *n*. **1**. a wooden handled tool with a metal head. **2**. a pointed tool.

pic nic /pik ′ nik/ *n*. a party or trip for which food is taken and eaten outside. **—***v*. **pic nicked**, **pic nick ing**. to go on or have a picnic. **—pic nick er**, *n*.

piece /pēs/ *n*. **1**. a part that has been broken, cut, or torn from something. **2**. one of a group or set of similar things. **3**. a work of art, music, or literature. **4**. an example or instance. **5**. a coin. **—***v*. **pieced**, **piec ing**. to join the parts of.

pi geon /pĭj ′ ən/ *n*. a bird that has a plump body, a small head, and thick, soft feathers.

pi lot /pī ′ lət/ *n*. **1**. a person who operates an aircraft or spacecraft. **2**. a person who steers large ships. **—***v*. to act as a pilot.

pi rate /pī ′ rit/ *n*. a person who robs ships at sea.

plaid /plad/ *n*. a pattern of stripes of different colors and widths crossing each other.

plain /plān/ *adj*. **1**. clearly seen, heard, or understood. **2**. straightforward; direct; frank. **3**. without decoration. **4**. not rich or highly seasoned. **5**. common or ordinary. **—***n*. an area of flat or almost flat land. **—plain ly**, *adv*. **—plain ness**, *n*.

plan /plan/ *n*. **1**. a way of doing something that has been thought out ahead of time. **2**. something that a person intends to do. **3**. a drawing that shows how the parts of some-

adj. adjective
adv. adverb
conj. conjunction
contr. contraction
def. definition
interj. interjection
n. noun
pl. plural
prep. preposition
pron. pronoun
sing. singular
v. verb
v.i. intransitive verb
v.t. transitive verb

thing are arranged. —v. **planned**, **plan ning**. 1. to think of a way of doing something ahead of time. 2. to have an intention, intend. 3. to make a drawing of. —**plan ner**, n.

plane[1] /plān/ n. 1. a level or grade. 2. an airplane. —adj. level or flat.

plane[2] /plān/ n. a hand tool with a sharp blade that sticks out from the bottom. —v. **planed**, **plan ing**. to smooth with a plane.

plan et /plan′ it/ n. one of nine large heavenly bodies that orbit the sun.

plas ma /plaz′ mə/ n. the clear, yellow liquid that forms the watery part of blood.

pleas ure /plezh′ ər/ n. 1. a feeling of enjoyment or happiness. 2. something that gives a feeling of enjoyment and happiness.

plen ty /plen′ tē/ n. a large amount; more than enough of something.

plow /plou/ n. a heavy farm tool.

pol lute /pə lüt′/ v. **pol lut ed**, **pol lut ing**. to make dirty or impure.

por cu pine /pôr kye pīn′/ n. a forest animal whose body is covered with sharp quills.

po si tion /pə zish′ ən/ n. 1. the place where a person or thing is. 2. a way of being placed. 3. a way of thinking about something. 4. rank; standing. 5. a job.

post pone /pōst pōn′/ v. **post poned**, **post pon ing**. to put off until later. —**post pone ment**, n.

po ta to /pə tā′ tō/ n., pl. **po ta toes**. the thick, rounded underground stem of a leafy plant.

pouch /pouch/ n., pl. **pouch es**. 1. a bag; sack. 2. a pocket of skin in some animals.

pour /pôr/ v. 1. to flow or cause to flow. 2. to rain hard. —**pour er**, n.

pow der /pou′ dər/ n. 1. fine bits made by crumbling something. 2. anything in the form of small dry particles. —v. 1. to make into fine bits. 2. to cover with fine bits.

praise /prāz/ n. words showing high regard and approval. —v. 1. to express high regard and approval of. 2. to worship. —**prais er**, n.

pre- a prefix that means before or ahead of time. *Prepaid* means paid for ahead of time.

pre fer /pri fûr′/ v. **pre ferred**; **pre fer ring**. to like better; choose above others.

pres i dent /prez′ i dənt/ n. 1. a person who is head of a government of a republic. 2. the person in charge of an organization.

pret ty /prit′ ē/ adj. **pret ti er**, **pret ti est**. sweetly pleasing, attractive, charming.

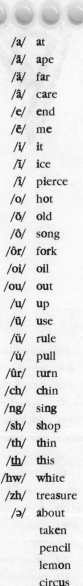

/a/	at
/ā/	ape
/ä/	far
/â/	care
/e/	end
/ē/	me
/i/	it
/ī/	ice
/î/	pierce
/o/	hot
/ō/	old
/ô/	song
/ôr/	fork
/oi/	oil
/ou/	out
/u/	up
/ū/	use
/ü/	rule
/ù/	pull
/ûr/	turn
/ch/	chin
/ng/	sing
/sh/	shop
/th/	thin
/th/	this
/hw/	white
/zh/	treasure
/ə/	about
	taken
	pencil
	lemon
	circus

pre view /prē ′ vū/ *n.* a showing of something ahead of time.

prom i nent /prom ′ ə nənt/ *adj.* 1. well-known or important. 2. noticeable. —**prom i nent ly**, *adv.*

prom ise /prom ′ is/ *n.* a statement which binds a person to do something. —*v.* to give one's word that something will be done.

pro mo tion /prə mō ′ shən/ *n.* a change to a higher rank, position, or grade. —**pro mo tion al**, *adj.*

prompt /prompt/ *adj.* quick or on time. —*v.* 1. to cause someone to do something. 2. to remind an actor of his lines.

pro nounce /prə nouns ′/ *v.* **pro nounced**, **pro nounc ing**. *v.* 1. to make the sound of a letter or word. 2. to say or declare. —**pro nounce able**, *adj.*

proof /prüf/ *n.* facts or evidence showing that something is true.

pro pel /prə pel ′/ *v.* **pro pelled, pro pel ling**. to cause to move forward or onward; put or keep in motion.

prop er /prop ər/ *adj.* 1. correct or suitable for a certain purpose or occasion. 2. thought of in a strict sense. *city proper.*

prove /prüv/ *v.* **proved, proved** or **prov en** /prü ven/, **prov ing**. 1. to

show that something is what it is supposed to be. 2. to have a certain result. —**prov a ble**, *adj.*

pur pose /pûr pəs/ *n.* the reason for which something is done.

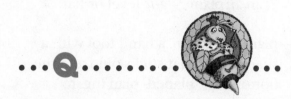

Q

quart /kwôrt/ *n.* a unit of measure that equals 2 pints or 1/4 of a gallon.

quest /kwest/ *n.* a search or pursuit.

quick /kwik/ *adj.* in a short time; fast. —**quick ness**, *n.*

quilt /kwilt/ *n.* a bed covering made of two pieces of cloth that are stuffed with soft material. —*v.* **quilt ed, quilt ing**. 1. to make a quilt or quilts. 2. to stitch together with a soft lining.

quote /kwōt/ *v.* **quot ed, quot ing**. to repeat the exact words of. —*n.* a quotation. —**quot er**, *n.*

R

ra dar /rā ′ där/ *n.* a device used to find and track objects.

ra di o /rā ′ dē o ′/ *n.* a way of sending sounds through the air without the use of wires.

rail way /rāl ′ wā ′/ *n.* **1.** a railroad. **2.** the tracks on which a train runs.

rain /rān/ *n.* water that falls in drops from clouds to the earth. —*v.* to fall in drops of water.

rain coat /rān ′ kōt ′/ *n.* a waterproof coat.

re- a prefix that means: **1.** again. *Reelect* means to elect again. **2.** back. *Recall* means to call back.

read /rēd/ *v.* **read** /red/, **read ing**. **1.** to look at and understand the meaning of. **2.** to say aloud something that is written. **3.** to give or show; register. *The thermometer read 70 degrees.*

real /rē ′ əl, rēl/ *adj.* **1.** actual or true; not imagined. **2.** genuine; not imitation.

rea son /rē ′ zən/ *n.* **1.** a cause or motive. **2.** the ability to think clearly. —*v.* **1.** to think about clearly. **2.** to try to change a person's mind. —**rea son er**, *n.*

re ceive /ri sēv ′/ *v.* **re ceived**, **re ceiv ing**. **1.** to take or get. **2.** to greet or welcome.

re cent /rē ′ sənt/ *adj.* happening not long ago. —**re cent ly**, *adv.* —**re cent ness**, *n.*

rec i pe /res ′ ə pē ′/ *n.* a list of ingredients and instructions for making something to eat or drink.

re cite /ri sīt ′/ *v.* **re cit ed**, **re cit ing**. **1.** to repeat something from memory. **2.** to tell the story of. —**re ci ter**, *n.*

reel /rēl/ *n.* a spool or similar device on which something is wound. —*v.* to wind on a reel.

reel /rēl/ *v.* to be thrown off balance; stagger.

re fer /ri fûr ′/ *v.* **re ferred**, **re fer ring**. **1.** to send or direct. **2.** to turn to for help or information. **3.** to call or direct attention.

ref er ee /ref ′ ə rē ′/ *n.* an official in games and sports who enforces the rules. —*v.* to act as a referee in.

re frig e ra tion /ri frij ′ ə rā ′ shən/ *n.* process of keeping something cool.

rein /rān/ *n.* **1.** one of two or more straps that are attached to a bridle or bit. **2.** any means of control.

rein deer /rān ′ dîr ′/ *n., pl.* **rein deer**. a large deer that has a white, gray, or brown coat and branching antlers.

re la tion /ri lā ′ shən/ *n.* a connection or dealings between one person or thing and another.

re mem ber /ri mem ′ bər/ *v.* **1.** to bring back to mind; recall. **2.** to keep in mind carefully.

rep re sent /rep ′ ri zent ′/ *v.* **1.** to stand for. **2.** to speak or act for.

/a/	at
/ā/	ape
/ä/	far
/â/	care
/e/	end
/ē/	me
/i/	it
/ī/	ice
/î/	pierce
/o/	hot
/ō/	old
/ô/	song
/ôr/	fork
/oi/	oil
/ou/	out
/u/	up
/ū/	use
/ü/	rule
/ù/	pull
/ûr/	turn
/ch/	chin
/ng/	sing
/sh/	shop
/th/	thin
/th/	this
/hw/	white
/zh/	treasure
/ə/	about
	taken
	pencil
	lemon
	circus

res i dent /rez ′ ə dənt/ *n.* a person who lives in a particular place.

re stric tion /ri strik ′ shən/ *n.* 1. something that restricts. 2. the act of restricting or the condition of being restricted.

re treat /ri trēt ′/ *v.* to draw or move back. —*n.* 1. the act of retreating. 2. a place in which to rest or relax.

rhyme /rīm/ *n.* the repetition of similar sounds at the ends of lines of verse. —*v.* **rhymed, rhym ing.** to make a rhyme.

rhy thm /rith ′ əm/ *n.* a regular or orderly repeating of sounds or movements.

road block /rōd ′ blok ′/ *n.* an obstacle; something standing in the way.

ro bot /rō ′ bət, rō ′ bot/ *n.* a machine that can do some of the things that a human can do.

rock et /rok ′ it/ *n.* a device that is driven through the air by a stream of hot gases that are released from the rear. —*v.* to move or rise very quickly.

ro de o /rō ′ dē o ′, rō dā ′ ō/ *n.* a show with contests in horseback riding, roping, and other skills.

rough /ruf/ *adj.* 1. having an uneven surface. 2. marked by force or violence. 3. in a natural or unfinished state. *rough diamonds.* 4. hard or unpleasant. *a rough day.* —*v.* to plan, sketch, or shape in an incomplete way. —**rough ly**, *adv.* —**rough ness**, *n.*

rou tine /rü tēn ′/ *n.* a regular way. —*adj.* according to or using routine. —**rou tine ly**, *adv.*

sal ad /sal ′ əd/ *n.* a cold dish that is made with vegetables. Meat, fish, eggs, or fruit are also used in salads.

san dal /san ′ dəl/ *n.* a shoe with a sole held to the foot by one or more straps.

sand wich /sand ′ wich, san ′ wich/ *n.,pl.* **sand wich es.** two or more slices of bread with a filling between them. —*v.* to fit or squeeze in tightly.

scrape /skrāp/ *v.* **scraped, scrap ing.** 1. to injure or scratch by rubbing against something. 2. to move with a sharp sound. 3. to clean or smooth by rubbing. —*n.* 1. a mark made on a surface by rubbing or scratching against something. 2. a harsh, grating sound. 3. a difficult, unpleasant situation.

scu ba /skü ′ bə/ *n.* special equipment which allows a swimmer to breathe underwater.

sea weed /sē ′ wēd ′/ *n.* a plant that grows in the sea, especially certain kinds of algae.

seize /sēz/ *v.* **seized, seiz ing**. **1.** to take hold of; grab. **2.** to get control of; capture.

se lec tion /si lek ʹ shən/ *n.* the selecting of a person or thing.

sense /səns/ *n.* **1.** a power of a living being to know about its surroundings and about changes in its own body. **2.** feeling. **3.** understanding or appreciation. **4.** intelligence. **5.** use; reason. —*v.* **sensed, sen sing.** to feel; understand.

sep a rate /*v.* sep ə rāt; *adj.* sep ʹ ər it or sep ʹ rit/ *v.* **sep a rated, sep a rat ing.** **1.** to keep apart; divide. **2.** to go in different directions. —*adj.* set apart; not joined. —**sep a rate ly**, *adv.*

Se quoi a /si kwoi ʹ ə/ *n.* a national park in central California.

ser geant /sär ʹ jənt/ *n.* an armed forces or police officer who is above a corporal or below a lieutenant.

sev er al /sev ʹ ər əl, sev ʹ rəl/ *adj.* more than two, but not many.

shall /shal/ *v.* an auxiliary verb that is used in the following ways: **1.** to express future actions. **2.** to express a requirement. **3.** to ask a question.

sham poo /sham pü ʹ/ *v.* to wash hair, rugs, or furniture coverings with a special soap. —*n.* a special soap used to wash hair, rugs, or furniture coverings.

sher iff /sher ʹ if/ *n.* the main officer responsible for enforcing the law in a county.

shop /shop/ *n.* a place where goods are sold or repaired. —*v.* **shopped, shop ping.** to visit stores in order to look at and buy goods.

shout /shout/ *v.* to call loudly; yell. —*n.* a loud call; yell. —**shout er**, *n.*

show /shō/ *v.* **showed, shown** or **showed, show ing.** **1.** to bring in sight or view. **2.** to make known. **3.** to point out or lead. **4.** to explain to. —*n.* something that is seen in public; display.

show er /shou ʹ ər/ *n.* **1.** a fall of anything in large numbers. **2.** a bath in which water is sprayed from overhead. **3.** a party where gifts are given to a future bride or a pregnant woman. —*v.* **1.** to rain or fall in a shower. **2.** to wet with water or another liquid. —**show er y**, *adj.*

shown /shōn/ *v.* a past participle of *show.*

sig nal /sig ʹ nəl/ *n.* **1.** something that warns, directs, or informs. **2.** an electric current that transmits sounds or pictures to receiving equipment. —*v.* to make a signal to. —*adj.* used as a signal.

sig nif i cant /sig nif ʹ i kənt/ *adj.* having special value or meaning; important.

/a/	at
/ā/	ape
/ä/	far
/â/	care
/e/	end
/ē/	me
/i/	it
/ī/	ice
/î/	pierce
/o/	hot
/ō/	old
/ô/	song
/ôr/	fork
/oi/	oil
/ou/	out
/u/	up
/ū/	use
/ü/	rule
/u̇/	pull
/ûr/	turn
/ch/	chin
/ng/	sing
/sh/	shop
/th/	thin
/th/	this
/hw/	white
/zh/	treasure
/ə/	about
	taken
	pencil
	lemon
	circus

si lence /si ′ ləns/ *n.* a lack of sound; complete quiet. —*v.* **si lenced, si lenc ing.** to make or keep silent.

sim ple /sim ′ pəl/ *adj.* **sim pler, sim plest.** easy to understand or do. —**simple ness,** *n.*

skel e ton /skel ′ i tən/ *n.* **1.** a framework that supports and protects the body of an animal. **2.** any framework or structure used as a support.

sketch /skech/ *n., pl.* **sketch es. 1.** a rough, quick drawing. **2.** a short piece of writing.

skull /skul/ *n.* the bony framework of the head in animals with a backbone.

sky line /skī ′ līn ′/ *n.* **1.** the outline of objects as seen against the sky. **2.** the line at which the earth and sky come together; horizon.

sky scrap er /skī ′ skrā pər/ *n.* a very tall building.

slay /slā/ *v.* **slew, slain, slay ing.** to kill in a violent way. *A brave knight slays a dragon.*

sleeve /slēv/ *n.* the part of a piece of clothing that covers all or part of the arm. —**sleeve less,** *adj.*

sleigh /slā/ *n.* a carriage on runners.

slum ber /slum ′ bər/ *v.* to sleep. —*n.* a sleep. —**slum ber er,** *n.*

smooth /smū<u>th</u>/ *adj.* **1.** having an even surface. **2.** able and skillful. —*v.*

1. make even or level. **2.** free from difficulty. —**smooth ly,** *adv.* —**smooth ness,** *n.*

snap shot /snap ′ shot ′/ *n.* an informal photograph.

sol dier /sōl ′ jer/ *n.* a person who is a member of an army.

sol emn /sol ′ əm/ *adj.* serious; grave. —**sol emn ly,** *adv.* —**sol emn ness,** *n.*

sol id /sol ′ id/ *adj.* **1.** having shape and hardness. **2.** of one material, color, or kind not mixed. **3.** not interrupted or broken. **4.** very strong; not weak. —*n.* a form of matter that has shape and hardness. —**sol id ly,** *adj.* —**sol id ness,** *n.*

so nar /sō ′ när/ *n.* an instrument that sends out waves to locate objects under the water.

soothe /sū<u>th</u>/ *v.* **soothed, sooth ing.** to quiet, calm, or ease. —**sooth er,** *n.*

soup /sūp/ *n.* a liquid food made by boiling meat, fish, or vegetables in water.

spar kle /spär ′ kəl/ *v.* **spar kled, spar kling. 1.** to shine in quick, bright flashes; glitter. **2.** to bubble. **3.** to be brilliant and lively. —*n.* a bright, glittering look.

spi nal cord /spī ′ nəl kôrd/ *n.* a thick cord of nerve tissue running through the center of the backbone.

splurge /splûrj/ *v.* **splurged, splurg ing**. to spend money freely.

spoil /spoil/ *v.* **spoiled** or **spoilt, spoil ing**. 1. to damage or hurt in some way. 2. to become so bad it cannot be eaten.

spurt /spûrt/ *v.* to pour out suddenly in a stream. —*n.* a sudden pouring out or bursting forth.

sta ble /stā ′ bəl/ *n.* a building where horses and cattle are kept and fed. —*v.* **sta bled, sta bling**. to put or keep in a stable.

sta ble /stā ′ bəl/ *adj.* not easily moved, shaken, or changed.

stad i um /stā ′ dē əm/ *n.* a structure made up of rows of seats built around an open field.

stale /stāl/ *adj.* **stal er, stal est**. 1. not fresh. 2. not new or interesting. —**stale ness**, *n.*

star tle /stär təl/ *v.* **star tled, star tling**. to excite or cause to move suddenly.

starve /stärv/ *v.* **starved, starv ing**. 1. to be very hungry. 2. to need or want very much.

stee ple /stē ′ pəl/ *n.* a high tower that narrows to a point and is built on a roof.

step /step/ *n.* 1. the movement of lifting the foot and putting it down again in a new position. 2. an action or stage in a series. —*v.* **stepped, step ping**. 1. to move by taking a step. 2. to put or press the foot.

steth o scope /steth ′ ə skōp/ *n.* an instrument used to listen to heartbeats and other sounds in the body.

stom ach /stum ′ ək/ *n.* a large muscular pouch that receives food and helps to break it down.

straight for ward /strāt ′ fôr ′ wərd/ *adj.* honest; truthful —**straight ly**, *adv.* —**straight ness**, *n.*

strength /strengkth, strength/ *n.* 1. the quality of being strong; energy, power. 2. the ability to take much strain. *the strength of the rope.*

stretch /strech/ *v.* to spread out to full length. —*n.* **stretch es**. 1. an unbroken space or area. *the stretch of road.* 2. the act of stretching.

stride /strīd/ *v.* **strode, strid den, strid ing**. to walk with long steps. —*n.* 1. a long step. 2. progress or improvement.

strike /strīk/ *v.* **struck, struck** or **strick en, strik ing**. 1. to give a blow to; hit. 2. to make an impression on. 3. to set on fire by rubbing or hitting. 4. to find or discover suddenly. 5. to stop work in order to get some improvement or benefit. —*n.* 1. the stopping of work. 2. a sudden discovery. 3. a baseball term.

strong /strông/ *adj.* 1. full of strength. 2. able to resist; firm. —**strong ly**, *adv.*

/a/	at
/ā/	ape
/ä/	far
/â/	care
/e/	end
/ē/	me
/i/	it
/ī/	ice
/î/	pierce
/o/	hot
/ō/	old
/ô/	song
/ôr/	fork
/oi/	oil
/ou/	out
/u/	up
/ū/	use
/ü/	rule
/ù/	pull
/ûr/	turn
/ch/	chin
/ng/	sing
/sh/	shop
/th/	thin
/th/	this
/hw/	white
/zh/	treasure
/ə/	about
	taken
	pencil
	lemon
	circus

175

struck /struk/ *v.* the past tense and past participle of *strike.*

struc ture /struk ′ chər/ *n.* **1.** anything that is built. **2.** an arrangement of parts. *structure of a plant cell.*

strug gle /strug ′ əl/ *v.* **strug gled, strug gling. 1.** to make a great effort. **2.** to fight; battle. —*n.* a great effort.

stub born /stub ′ ərn/ *adj.* **1.** not yielding. **2.** hard to overcome or deal with.

stu dent /stü ′ dənt/ *n.* a person who is studying something.

adj.	adjective
adv.	adverb
conj.	conjunction
contr.	contraction
def.	definition
interj.	interjection
n.	noun
pl.	plural
prep.	preposition
pron.	pronoun
sing.	singular
v.	verb
v.i.	intransitive verb
v.t.	transitive verb

stud i o /stü ′ dē ō ′, stū ′ dē ō ′/ *n.* **1.** a place where an artist or craftsperson works. **2.** a place where motion pictures are filmed.

stud y /stud ′ ē/ *v.* **stud ied, stud y ing. 1.** to try to learn by reading, thinking, or observing. **2.** to look at closely; examine. —*n.* **stud ies. 1.** the act of studying. **2.** a close look at something; examination. **3.** a room used for studying.

stum ble /stum ′ bəl/ *v.* **stum bled, stum bling. 1.** to lose one's balance; trip. **2.** to move or speak in a clumsy way. **3.** to discover by chance. —**stum bling ly,** *adv.*

style /stīl/ *n.* **1.** a particular way of saying or doing something. **2.** fashion.

sub mar ine /*n.* sub ′ mə rēn ′; *adj.* sub ′ mə rēn ′/ **1.** a ship that can travel under water. **2.** a sandwich made with one long loaf of bread.

sun glass es /sun ′ glas ′ iz/ *pl., n.* a pair of dark pieces of glass or plastic in a frame that help protect the eyes from the glare of the sun.

sup pose /sə pōz ′/ *v.* **sup posed, sup pos ing. 1.** to imagine to be possible. **2.** to believe; guess.

sur face /sûr ′ fis/ *n.* **1.** the outside of a thing. **2.** outer look or appearance. —*adj.* of or having to do with a surface. —*v.* **sur faced, sur fac ing.** to come or rise to the surface.

surf board /sûrf ′ bôrd ′/ *n.* a long, flat board used to ride on the crest of a wave.

sur name /sûr ′ nāme ′/ *n.* a last name; family name.

sur plus /sûr ′ plus ′/ *n.* an amount greater than what is used or needed. —*adj.* greater than what is needed.

swal low¹ /swol ′ ō/ *v.* **1.** to cause food to pass from the mouth to the stomach. **2.** to take or keep back. *Swallow your pride.* —*n.* the act of swallowing. —**swal low er,** *n.*

swal low² /swol ′ ō/ *n.* a small bird with long wings.

sweat er /swet ′ ər/ *n.* a warm, knitted piece of clothing worn over the upper part of the body.

sweat shirt /swet ′ shûrt / *n.* a heavy, knitted shirt that usually has long sleeves and no collar.

sweep /swēp/ *v.* **swept, sweep ing.** 1. to clean with a broom or brush. 2. to move and carry quickly and forcefully. —*n.* any quick, sweeping motion.

swept /swept/ *v.* past tense and past participle of *sweep.*

sword /sôrd/ *n.* a weapon that has a long, sharp blade set in a handle. —**sword like**, *adj.*

syr up /sir ′ əp, sûr ′ əp/ *n.* a thick, sweet liquid. —**syr up like**, *adj.*

sys tem /sis təm/ *n.* 1. a group of things that form a whole. 2. a group of laws, beliefs, or facts. 3. an orderly method.

• • • **T** • • • • • • • • • • • • • •

ta ble spoon /tā ′ bəl spün / *n.* a large spoon that is used to serve and mea-sure food.

take /tāk/ *v.* **took, tak en, tak ing.** 1. to get a hold of; grasp. 2. to capture or win by using force or skill. 3. to obtain; get.

tar get /tär ′ git/ *n.* 1. a mark or object that is aimed at. 2. a person or thing that is made fun of or criticized.

taught /tôt/ *v.* past tense and past par-ticiple of *teach.*

teach /tēch/ *v.* **taught, teach ing.** to give knowledge to, especially through lessons or formal schooling; instruct.

team mate /tēm ′ māt ′/ *n.* a person who is a member of a team.

tea spoon /tē ′ spün ′/ *n.* a spoon that is used to eat with and to measure food.

tel e graph /tel ′ i graf ′/ *n.* a system or equipment used for sending mes-sages by wire over a long distance.

tel e phone /tel ′ ə fōn ′/ *n.* a system or instrument used to send sound over a long distance. *v.* **tel e phoned, tel e phon ing** to talk with someone by telephone.

tel e vi sion /tel ′ ə vizh ′ ən/ *n.* 1. a system for sending and receiving pic-tures and sound over long distances by means of electricity. 2. a set or device on which these pictures are seen and the sound is heard.

ten don /ten ′ dən/ *n.* a strong cord or band of tissue that attaches a mus-cle to a bone or other part of the body.

ten nis /ten ′ is/ *n.* a game in which two or four players hit a small ball over a net with a racket.

their /thâr/ *pron.* of, belonging to, or having to do with them.

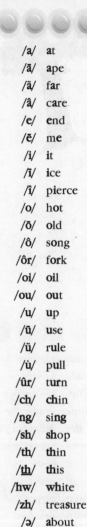

/a/	at
/ā/	ape
/ä/	far
/â/	care
/e/	end
/ē/	me
/i/	it
/ī/	ice
/î/	pierce
/o/	hot
/ō/	old
/ô/	song
/ôr/	fork
/oi/	oil
/ou/	out
/u/	up
/ū/	use
/ü/	rule
/u̇/	pull
/ûr/	turn
/ch/	chin
/ng/	sing
/sh/	shop
/th/	thin
/th/	this
/hw/	white
/zh/	treasure
/ə/	about
	taken
	pencil
	lemon
	circus

there /th̲âr/ *adv.* at, in, or to that place. —*n.* that place. *interj.* a word used to express satisfaction or sympathy.

think /thingk/ *v.* **thought, think ing.** 1. to use the mind to form ideas and to make decisions. 2. to call to mind or remember. —**think er**, *n.*

thirst /thûrst/ *n.* 1. an uncomfortable feeling of dryness in the mouth and throat. 2. a strong desire for something.

thought /thôt/ *v.* past tense and past participle of *think*. —*n.* 1. the act of thinking. 2. careful consideration.

thou sand /thou zend/ *n., adj.* ten times a hundred; 1,000.

thrift /thrift/ *n.* careful management of money or anything valuable. —**thrift y**, *adj.*

throat /thrōt/ *n.* 1. the passage in the body between the mouth and the esophagus. 2. the front of the neck.

throne /thrōn/ *n.* 1. the chair occupied by the king and queen at ceremonies. 2. the power or authority of a king or queen.

throw /thrō/ *v.* **threw, thrown, throw ing.** 1. to send up into or through the air. 2. to make fall to the ground. —*n.* the act of throwing; toss. —**throw er**, *n.*

thrown /thrōn/ *v.* past participle of *throw.*

thumb /thum/ *n.* 1. the short, thick finger on the hand. 2. the part of a mitten or glove that covers the thumb. —*v.* to turn and look through pages quickly.

thun der /thun ′ dər/ *n.* a loud rumbling or crackling sound that follows lightning. —*v.* to make thunder or a noise that is like thunder.

tide /tīd/ *n.* the regular rise and fall of the water level of large bodies of water that is caused by the pull of the moon and sun on the earth.

tie /tī/ *v.* **tied, ty ing.** 1. to fasten or attach with a bow or knot. 2. to draw together or join closely. —*n.* 1. a cord, string, or line that is used to fasten things together. 2. a strip of cloth that is worn around the neck; necktie.

tis sue /tish ′ ü/ *n.* a group of cells in a plant or animal that are similar in form and in function.

ti tle /tī ′ təl/ *n.* 1. the name of a work of art. 2. a word or a group of words used to show a person's status, rank, or occupation. 3. a championship.

toe /tō/ *n.* 1. one of the slender parts that stick out from a foot. 2. the parts of socks or shoes that cover the toes.

tol er ant /tol ′ ər ənt/ *adj.* willing to respect or try to understand customs, ideas, or beliefs that are different from one's own. —**tol er ant ly**, *adv.*

adj.	adjective
adv.	adverb
conj.	conjunction
contr.	contraction
def.	definition
interj.	interjection
n.	noun
pl.	plural
prep.	preposition
pron.	pronoun
sing.	singular
v.	verb
v.i.	intransitive verb
v.t.	transitive verb

to ma to /tə mā ′ tō/ *n., pl.* **to ma toes.**
1. the round, juicy fruit of a plant.
2. the plant that produces this fruit.

tongue /tung/ *n.* **1.** a movable piece
of flesh in the mouth. **2.** an animal's
tongue cooked and used for food.
3. a language. *Spanish is her native
tongue.*

ton sil /ton ′ səl/ *n.* either of two
small, oval pieces of flesh in the
throat at the back of the mouth.

touch /tuch/ *v.* **1.** to put a part of the
body on or against something. **2.** to
bring something against something
else. **3.** to affect a person's feelings or
emotions. —*n.* **touch es.** **1.** the sense
by which a person becomes aware of
things by feeling or handling. **2.** the
act of touching. ′

tough /tuf/ *adj.* **1.** not easy to break,
cut, or damage; strong. **2.** able to put
up with difficulty, strain, or hardship.
3. demanding. —**tough ly**, *adv.*
—**tough ness**, *n.*

tow el /tou ′ əl/ *n.* a piece of paper or
cloth that is used for wiping or dry-
ing something. —*v.* to wipe or dry
with a towel.

trace /trās/ *n.* a small sign left behind
showing that something was there.
—*v.* **traced, trac ing.** **1.** to follow the
trail, course, or path of. **2.** to copy by
following lines. —**trace able**, *adj.*

trac tor /trak ′ tər/ *n.* a vehicle with
heavy tires or tracks.

tra di tion /trə dish ′ ən/ *n.* the practice of passing down customs, beliefs,
or other knowledge from parents to
their children.

tran sis tor /tran zis ′ tər/ *n.* a very
small electronic device that controls
the electric current in television sets
and other equipment.

trans par ent /trans pâr ′ ənt,
trans par ′ ənt/ *adj.* **1.** allowing things
to pass through so that things on the
other side can be easily seen. **2.** easy
to understand. —**trans par ent ly**, *adv.*
—**trans par ent ness**, *n.*

trav el /trav ′ əl/ *v.* **trav eled, trav el ing.**
to go from one place to another. —*n.*
the act of traveling.

treas ure /trezh ′ ər/ *n.* objects that
are valuable. —*v.* **treas ured,
treas ur ing.** to think of as being of
great value or importance.

trem ble /trem ′ bəl/ *v.* **trem bled,
trem bling.** **1.** to shake with cold, fear,
weakness, or anger. **2.** to move or
vibrate. —**trem bling ly**, *adv.* —**trem bly**,
adj.

tri al /trī ′ əl/ *n.* **1.** the examination of
a person accused of a crime in a
court of law. **2.** a trying or testing of
something. **3.** hardship.

tri cer a tops /trī ser ′ ə tops / *n., pl.*
tri cer a top ses. a dinosaur that had a
long horn over each eye, a short horn
on its snout, and a bony collar over
the back of its head.

/a/ at
/ā/ ape
/ä/ far
/â/ care
/e/ end
/ē/ me
/i/ it
/ī/ ice
/î/ pierce
/o/ hot
/ō/ old
/ô/ song
/ôr/ fork
/oi/ oil
/ou/ out .
/u/ up
/ū/ use
/ü/ rule
/ù/ pull
/ûr/ turn
/ch/ chin
/ng/ sing
/sh/ shop
/th/ thin
/th/ this
/hw/ white
/zh/ treasure
/ə/ about
taken
pencil
lemon
circus

tri umph /trī ′ umf/ *n.* **1.** a great success or victory. **2.** great happiness caused by success or victory. —*v.* to succeed or win.

tri um phant /trī um ′ fənt/ *adj.* successful or victorious. —**tri um phant ly**, *adv.*

trom bone /trom bōn ′, trom ′ bōn/ *n.* a brass musical instrument with a long slide for changing tones. —**trom bon ist**, *n.*

troop /trüp/ *n.* a group of persons doing something together. —*v.* to walk or march in a group.

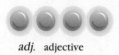

adj.	adjective
adv.	adverb
conj.	conjunction
contr.	contraction
def.	definition
interj.	interjection
n.	noun
pl.	plural
prep.	preposition
pron.	pronoun
sing.	singular
v.	verb
v.i.	intransitive verb
v.t.	transitive verb

trou ble /trub ′ əl/ *n.* **1.** a difficult or dangerous situation. **2.** extra work or effort. —*v.* **trou bled, trou bling. 1.** to disturb or make uncomfortable. **2.** to cause someone to make an extra effort.

trou ble mak er /trub ′ əl mā ′ kər/ *n.* a person who is a cause of trouble.

trough /trôf/ *n.* a long, deep, narrow box or other container to hold food for animals.

true /trü/ *adj.* **tru er, tru est. 1.** agreeing with the facts; not false. **2.** loyal. **3.** genuine. —**true ness**, *n.*

trum pet /trum ′ pit/ *n.* a brass musical instrument with valves and a flared bell. —**trum pet er**, *n.*

truth /trüth/ *n.* **1.** something that is true. **2.** the quality of being true, honest, or sincere.

tur key /tûr ′ kē/ *n.* a large North American bird with black and brown feathers and a tail shaped like a fan.

tur moil /tûr ′ moil/ *n.* great confusion or disorder.

type writ er /tīp ′ rī tər/ *n.* a machine with keys for each letter of the alphabet, numbers, and punctuation marks.

ty phoon /tī fün ′/ *n.* a tropical storm with violent winds.

typ i cal /tip ′ i kəl/ *adj.* showing the qualities or characteristics of a certain type.

• • • **U** • • • • • • • • •  • • •

un- a prefix that means the opposite of; not. *Unexpected* means not expected.

un cle /ung ′ kəl/ *n.* **1.** the brother of one's mother or father. **2.** the husband of one's aunt.

un der brush /un dər brush ′/ *n.* bushes and other plants growing under big trees in a forest or woods.

u nite /ū nīt ′/ *v.* **u nit ed, u nit ing.** to bring or join together; make or become one.

ur ban /ûr ′ bən/ *adj.* in, having to do with, or like a city or city life.

u su al /ū ′ zhü əl/ *adj.* common or expected; customary.

veg e ta ble /vej ′ i tə bəl, vej ′ tə bəl/ *n.* a plant whose roots, leaves, or other parts are used as food. —*adj.* having to do with or made from vegetables or other plants.

vein /vān/ *n.* 1. one of the blood vessels that carry blood from all parts of the body to the heart. 2. one of the stiff tubes that form the framework of a leaf or an insect's wing.

ver sion /vûr ′ zhən/ *n.* 1. an account or description given from a particular point of view. 2. a translation from one language to another.

ver te bra /vûr ′ tə brə/ *n.*, *pl.*, **ver te brae** /vûr ′ tə bre /, **ver te bras**. one of the small bones that make up the backbone.

vil lain /vil ′ ən/ *n.* a wicked or evil person.

vis it /viz ′ it/ *v.* 1. to go or come to see. 2. to stay with as a guest. —*n.* a short stay or call.

vol ume /vol ′ ūm/ *n.* 1. a book. 2. one of a set or series of related books or magazines. 3. the amount of space occupied. 4. the amount of sound.

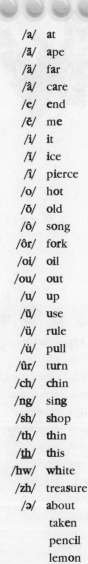

wade /wād/ **wad ed**, **wad ing**. *v.* 1. to walk in or through water or mud. 2. to make one's way slowly and with difficulty.

waf fle /wof ′ əl/ *n.* a crisp cake made of batter.

wag /wag/ *v.* **wagged**, **wag ging**. to move quickly from side to side or up and down. —*n.* the act of wagging.

wait /wāt/ *v.* 1. to stay in a place until someone comes or something happens. 2. to be put off or delayed. —*n.* the act of waiting.

wait er /wā ′ tər/ *n.* a man whose job is serving food or drink.

-ward a suffix that means in the direction of. *Downward* means to move down.

warm /wôrm/ *adj.* 1. somewhat hot; not cold. 2. having a feeling of heat in or on the body. 3. giving off heat. —*v.* 1. to make warm or heated. 2. to fill with friendly feelings.—**warm ly**, *adv.* —**warm ness**, *n.*

/a/	at
/ā/	ape
/ä/	far
/â/	care
/e/	end
/ē/	me
/i/	it
/ī/	ice
/î/	pierce
/o/	hot
/ō/	old
/ô/	song
/ôr/	fork
/oi/	oil
/ou/	out
/u/	up
/ū/	use
/ü/	rule
/ u̇/	pull
/ûr/	turn
/ch/	chin
/ng/	sing
/sh/	shop
/th/	thin
/th/	this
/hw/	white
/zh/	treasure
/ə/	about
	taken
	pencil
	lemon
	circus

181

watch /woch/ *v.* **1.** to look at carefully. **2.** to guard. **3.** to look in a careful, alert way. —*n.* **1.** the act of looking carefully. **2.** a device that measures and shows the time. —**watch er**, *n.*

wa ter fall /wô ′ tər fôl ′/ *n.* a natural stream of water falling from a high place.

weath er /we<u>th</u> ′ ər/ *n.* the condition of the air or atmosphere at a particular time and place. —*v.* to cause to be dried, bleached, or aged by the weather.

adj.	adjective
adv.	adverb
conj.	conjunction
contr.	contraction
def.	definition
interj.	interjection
n.	noun
pl.	plural
prep.	preposition
pron.	pronoun
sing.	singular
v.	verb
v.i.	intransitive verb
v.t.	transitive verb

weed /wēd/ *n.* a useless or harmful plant. —*v.* to take out the weeds.

weigh /wā/ *v.* **1.** to find out the weight or heaviness. **2.** to think about or examine carefully.

weight /wāt/ *n.* **1.** the amount or heaviness. **2.** the quality of a thing that comes from the pull of gravity upon it. **3.** units for expressing weight.

wel come /wel ′ kəm/ *v.* **1.** to greet someone in a pleasant, friendly way. **2.** to receive or accept with pleasure.

wheel /hwēl, wēl/ *n.* **1.** a round frame or solid object. —*v.* to turn. **2.** to move or roll on wheels.

wheth er /hwe<u>th</u> ′ ər, we<u>th</u> ′ ər/ *conj.* **1.** a word that is used to introduce a choice between things. **2.** if.

whis per ing /hwis ′ pər, wis ′ pər/ *v.* to speak or say very softly. —*n.* a very soft way of speaking. —**whis per er**, *n.*

whis tle /hwis ′ əl, wis ′ əl/ *v.* **whis tled**, **whis tling**. to make a clear, sharp sound by forcing air out through rounded lips or through the teeth. —*n.* **1.** a device that makes a clear, sharp sound when air is blown through it. **2.** a whistling sound. —**whis tler**, *n.*

width /width, with/ *n.* the distance from one side of something to the other side.

wo man /wûm ′ ən/ *n., pl.* **wom en.** **1.** an adult female person. **2.** adult female people as a group.

won't /wōnt/ *contr.* shortened form of "will not."

word /wûrd/ *n.* **1.** a sound having meaning and forming a unit of the language. **2.** a written or printed letter or letters standing for such a sound. **3.** a short conversation or statement. —*v.* to put into words.

would n't /wûd ′ ənt/ *contr.* shortened form of "would not."

wreck /rek/ *v.* to destroy or ruin. —*n.* what is left from something that has been ruined or damaged.

wrench /rench/ *n. pl.*, **wrench es.** **1.** a very hard, sharp twist or pull. **2.** a tool with jaws. —*v.* to twist or pull with a hard, sharp motion.

wres tle /res ˈ əl/ *v.* **wres tled**, **wres tling**. 1. to struggle by grasping and trying to force the opponent on the ground without punching. 2. to struggle very hard. —**wres tler**, *n.*

wring /ring/ *v.* **wrung**, **wring ing**. 1. to squeeze or twist so that liquid is forced out. 2. to get by force.

wrin kle /ring ˈ kəl/ *n.* a small fold, ridge, or line in a smooth surface. —*v.* **wrin kled**, **wrin kling**. to make or have a fold, ridge, or line in a smooth surface.

writ ing /rī ˈ ting/ *n.* 1. letters, words, or symbols that are written by hand. 2. a book or play that has been written. 3. the act of making letters.

yard [1] /yärd/ *n.* 1. an area of ground next to a building. 2. an enclosed area.

yard [2] /yärd/ *n.* 1. a measure of length equal to 36 inches. 2. a rod fastened across the mast of a ship to hold a sail.

year /yîr/ *n.* 1. a period of time made up of twelve months. 2. a part of a year spent in a particular activity. *a school year.*

Yo sem i te /yō sem ˈ ə tē/ *n.* a national park in eastern California.

you'd /ūd/ *contr.* shortened form of "you had" or "you would."

young /yung/ *adj.* in the early part of life or growth. —*n.* young offspring. —**young ness**, *n.*

Y

-y a suffix that is often added to a noun to form an adjective and that means: 1. full of; having. *Dirty* means full of dirt. 2. like. *Wintry* means like winter. 3. tending to. *Sticky* means tending to stick.

Z

ze ro /zîr ˈ ō/ *n., pl.,* **ze ros, ze roes**. *adj.* 1. the number 0, which means no quantity or amount at all. 2. a point on a scale at which numbering begins or measurement begins. —*adj.* 1. of, being, or at zero. 2. none at all; not any.

/a/	at
/ā/	ape
/ä/	far
/â/	care
/e/	end
/ē/	me
/i/	it
/ī/	ice
/î/	pierce
/o/	hot
/ō/	old
/ô/	song
/ôr/	fork
/oi/	oil
/ou/	out
/u/	up
/ū/	use
/ü/	rule
/ù/	pull
/ûr/	turn
/ch/	chin
/ng/	sing
/sh/	shop
/th/	thin
/th/	this
/hw/	white
/zh/	treasure
/ə/	about
	taken
	pencil
	lemon
	circus

STUDENT NOTES

STUDENT NOTES

STUDENT NOTES

STUDENT NOTES

STUDENT NOTES

LESSON 1

Focus
page 2

1–15. jazz, cancel, lantern, blanket, tractor, travel, shampoo, paddle, castle, magnet, salad, palace, catalog, cabin, cabinet
16–19. handsome, handicap, anchor, casserole
20. plaid

Words and Meanings
page 3

1. magnet
2. castle/palace
3. cabin
4. lantern
5. shampoo
6. salad
7. catalog
8. travel
9. paddle
10. blanket
11. tractor
12. cabinet
13. jazz
14. palace/castle
15. cancel

Word Works

16. canceled
17. traveling
18. preferring
19. propelled
20. offering

Word Play
page 4

1–3. palace, cabinet, blanket
4–6. magnet, catalog, salad

7. jazz
8. tractor
9. cabin
10. lantern
11. shampoo
12–13. paddle, castle
14–15. cancel, travel
16. cabin
17. cabinet
18. cancel
19. castle
20. catalog

Write on Your Own
page 5

The Write on Your Own activities need not always result in finished or published writing. Often it is more productive to focus on a particular aspect of good writing and allow students to experiment with various revisions without having them rewrite for submission and evaluation.

Song words will vary. Students should use four Core Words. For peer evaluation, have students sing/say their songs.

Proofreading Practice

1–4. blanket, salad, cancel, travel

LESSON 2

Focus
page 6

1–9. bench, swept, kennel, plenty, welcome, tennis, sense, quest, enemy
10–15. health, feather, meant, sweater, breath, leather
16–20. necessary, centipede, president, pennant, vegetables

Words and Meanings
page 7

1. quest
2. health
3. welcome
4. plenty
5. meant
6. sense
7. enemy
8. swept
9. feather
10. sweater
11. leather
12. breath
13. kennel
14. tennis
15. bench

Word Works

16–18. mean/meant, sweep/swept, teach/taught

Word Play
page 8

1. Kennel
2. Health
3. Sweater
4. Bench
5. Leather
6. Tennis
7. swept
8. quest
9. plenty
10. enemy
11. breath
12. feather
13. welcome
14. meant
15. sense

Write on Your Own
page 9

Paragraphs will vary. Students should use four Core Words.

To help students organize their thoughts, you might ask them to list three activities in order of importance as a prewriting exercise. Check drafts for a logical order of thought.

Proofreading Practice

1–4. health, plenty, breath, sense
5. This
6. exercise.

LESSON 3

Focus
page 10

1–7. collar, comet, congress, proper, common, prompt, promise
8–15. cause, awful, though, broad, caught, fought, bought, ought
16–20. modern, colony, crocodile, trombone, honest

Words and Meanings
page 11

1. bought
2. prompt
3. broad
4. congress
5. thought
6. fought
7. awful
8. caught
9. cause
10. promise
11. proper
12. common
13. collar
14. ought
15. comet

Word Works

Answers may vary slightly.

16. not proper
17. not common
18. do not obey
19. do not trust
20. not complete

Word Play
page 12

1. cause
2. prompt
3. broad
4. caught
5. awful
6. proper
7. common
8. promise
9. collar
10. comet
11. congress
12. thought
13. fought
14. bought
15. ought
16. think
17. bring
18. catch
19. fight
20. buy

Write on Your Own
page 13

News stories will vary. Students should use four Core Words.

Check the news stories to see if students have included answers to the who, what, where, and why questions that news stories usually cover in the lead paragraph.

Proofreading Practice

1–5. caught, prompt, awful, cause, ought

LESSON 4

Focus
page 14

1–10. glimpse, igloo, limit, blizzard, whistle, imitate, width, simple, visit, thrift
11–12. quilt, built
13–15. mystery, myth, system
16–20. instinct, typical, biscuit, gymnast, mischief

Words and Meanings
page 15

1. myth
2. visit
3. glimpse
4. igloo
5. built
6. mystery
7. simple
8. limit
9. thrift
10. imitate
11. system
12. width
13. blizzard
14. whistle
15. quilt

Word Works

16. mysterious
17. thrifty
18. mighty
19. glorious
20. fruity

Word Play
page 16

1. width
2. quilt
3. limit
4. igloo
5. visit
6. blizzard
7. whistle
8. mystery
9. simple
10. system
11. myth
12. built
13. glimpse
14. thrift
15. imitate

Write on Your Own
page 17

Descriptions will vary. Students should use four Core Words.

This description offers an opportunity to have students work on writing fresh and interesting similes. When students have completed the assignment, ask them to use their descriptions to write a new ending for the sentence, "Snow covered the ground like a ...."

Proofreading Practice

1–5. blizzard, quilt, mystery, whistle, visit
6. December
7. Jabal
8–9. Mr.

LESSON 5

Focus
page 18
1–9. study, clumsy, trumpet, hunger, thunder, bundle, bumblebee, chuckle, struggle
10–13. glove, none, honey, money
14–15. trouble, country
16–20. j(u)stice, g(o)vern, c(u)stomer, sl(u)mber, str(u)cture

Words and Meanings
page 19
1. country
2. trumpet
3. hunger
4. none
5. bundle
6. trouble
7. thunder
8. bumblebee
9. study
10. money
11. honey
12. glove
13. chuckle
14. clumsy
15. struggle

Word Works
16. country
17. bundle
18. chuckle
19. hunger
20. money
21. none
22. study
23. struggle
24. clumsy

Word Play
page 20
1. clumsy
2. struggle
3. hunger
4. bundle
5. bumblebee
6. country
7. trumpet
8. study
9. trouble
10. thunder
11. money
12. glove
13. chuckle
14. honey
15. none
16. a room used for studying
17. to have a strong wish or need for something
18. a noise that is like thunder
19. the land outside of cities and towns
20. a very dear person or thing

Write on Your Own
page 21
Thank-you notes will vary. Students should use four Core Words.

The class could write thank-you letters to someone who has done a favor for the school.

Proofreading Practice
1–4. trouble, country, study, struggle

REVIEW LESSON 6

1. shampoo
2. cabin
3. blanket
4. tractor
5. sense
6. quest
7. sweater
8. swept
9. promise
10. common
11. broad
12. awful
13. igloo
14. width
15. mystery
16. blizzard
17. money
18. glove
19. study
20. trouble

LESSON 7

Focus
page 24
1–15. scrape, hast(y), br(ie)f, favor, s(ei)ze, danger, b(ea)ver, reind(ee)r, retr(ea)t, reins, stale, sleigh, sl(ee)ves, great, pr(ai)se
16–20. (teammate), ache, relation, receive, maintain

Words and Meanings
page 25
1. praise
2. great
3. brief
4. hasty
5. danger
6. favor
7. seize
8. scrape
9. stale
10. sleeves
11. retreat
12. reins
13. sleigh
14. reindeer
15. beaver

Word Works
16. grate
17. great
18. sleigh
19. Slay
20. rains
21. reins

Word Play
page 26
1. scrape
2. stale
3. sleeves
4. sleigh
5. great
6. beaver
7. retreat
8. favor
9. hasty
10. danger
11–12. reindeer, reins
13–14. brief, seize
15. praise

Write on Your Own
page 27
Stories will vary. Students should use four Core Words.

You might wish to have students focus on writing a good beginning for their stories, one that will make the reader want to read further. One strategy is to have students draft three possible openings and share them with a partner before deciding on the best opening sentence.

Proofreading Practice
1–5. beaver, danger, great, brief, seize

LESSON 8

Focus***
page 28
1–15. qu(o)t(e), lightning, r(o)bot, b(oa)st, skyline, h(o)tel, climate, gr(ow)th, lifeb(oa)t, (o)vergr(ow)n, stri(de), p(o)stp(o)n(e), m(o)tor, idea, reci(te)
16–20. typewriter, b(ou)lder, silence, alth(ough), (ow)nership

Words and Meanings
page 29
1. postpone
2. hotel
3. stride
4. idea
5. boast/quote
6. climate
7. growth
8. lightning
9. skyline
10. robot
11. motor
12. lifeboat
13. overgrown
14. recite
15. quote

Word Works
Definitions may vary.
16. overgrown, "grown over"
17. lifeboat, "a boat for saving lives"
18. skyline, "the outline of buildings against the sky"
19. firefly, "a bug that flashes light"
20. backbone, "spine"

Word Play
page 30
1. motor
2. climate
3. lightning
4. growth
5. postpone
6. skyline
7. recite
8. hotel
9. lifeboat
10. robot
11. overgrown
12. stride
13. boast
14. quote
15. idea
16–18. growth, hotel, idea

Write on Your Own
page 31
Diary entries will vary. Students should use four Core Words.

You might have part of the class describe the day on the boat from the point of view of an observer using he, she, and they instead of the I and we of the first-person approach in a diary.

Proofreading Practice
1–4. hotel, idea, overgrown, boast
5. July 15, 1993
6. Our
7. whale.

LESSON 9

Focus
page 32
NOTE: The first syllable of the Challenge Word *nuisance* can be pronounced /nü/ or /nū/.
1–15. s(ou)p, (u)s(u)al, pr(o)v(e), (u)nite, cr(ui)se, music, l(u)nar, cart(oo)n, cl(ue), tiss(ue), s(oo)thing, tr(u)th, n(oo)dle, sc(u)ba, sm(oo)th
16–20. junior, museum, routine, preview, (nuisance)

Words and Meanings
page 33
1. cruise
2. scuba
3. truth
4. prove
5. clue
6. cartoon
7. usual
8. smooth
9. noodle
10. soup
11. lunar
12. soothing
13. tissue
14. music
15. unite

Word Works
16. usually
17. soothingly
18. smoothly
19. clumsily
20. properly
21. commonly
22. promptly
23. hastily
24. awfully

Word Play
page 34
1–5. usual, music, lunar, cruise, soothing
6. soup
7. prove
8. truth
9. clue
10. scuba
11. unite
12. cartoon
13. smooth
14. tissue
15. noodle

Write on Your Own
page 35
Advertisements will vary. Students should use four Core Words.

Have students brainstorm a series of effective adjectives to describe the sport of scuba diving. Write them on the board and urge students to use the ones they like best in their drafts. Check advertisements for effective use of adjectives.

Proofreading Practice
1–4. usual, cruise, soothing, clue
5. vacation?
6. thrill!
7. August

LESSON 10

Focus
page 36
1–4. b(ur)nt, ch(ur)n, sp(ur)t, spl(ur)ge
5–15. (ur)ban, occ(ur) b(ur)den, h(ur)dle, f(ur)nace, p(ur)pose, s(ur)plus, t(ur)key, f(ur)nish, t(ur)moil, c(ur)rent
16–20. journal, journey, surname, courtesy, surfboard

Words and Meanings
page 37
1. hurdle
2. burden
3. occur
4. turmoil
5. furnish
6. spurt
7. surplus
8. purpose
9. current
10. urban
11. churn
12. furnace
13. splurge
14. turkey
15. burnt

Word Works
Definitions may vary slightly.
16. rewrite, "write again"
17. redial, "dial again"
18. rebuild, "build again"
19. rehire, "hire again"
20. restate, "state again"

Word Play
page 38
1. hurdle
2. purpose
3. occur
4. burden
5. splurge
6. churn
7. spurt
8. current/burnt
9. burnt
10. furnish
11. turkey
12. urban
13. surplus
14. turmoil
15. furnace
16. oc/cur
17. fur/nish
18. hur/dle
19. fur/nace
20. bur/den

Write on Your Own
page 39
Descriptions will vary. Students should use four Core Words.

Focus on having students choose interesting details in their descriptions of the lives of the early settlers. Then check drafts for detailed descriptions.

Proofreading Practice
1–5. turmoil, burnt, surplus, purpose, burden

LESSON 11

Focus
page 40
NOTE: Students may circle different unusual spellings. These are possible answers.
1–4. lo(s)e, cor(p)s, tong(ue), b(ei)ge
5–12. s(y)rup, b(u)sy, d(o)zen, ang(el), ang(le), ma(ch)ine, bu(s)iness, h(o)n(or)
13–15. d(ia)ry, recip(e), sep(a)rate
16–20. (ch)ord, (on)ion, sol(d)ier, sheri(ff), serg(ea)nt

Words and Meanings
page 41
1. tongue
2. honor
3. separate
4. angle
5. beige
6. busy
7. machine
8. syrup
9. recipe
10. lose
11. angel
12. diary
13. dozen
14. corps
15. business

Word Works
16. busier
17. tallest
18. fluffiest
19. newer
20. prettiest

Word Play
page 42
1. lose
2. busy
3. recipe
4. diary
5. dozen
6. corps
7. tongue
8. honor
9. business
10–11. angel, angle
12. beige
13. separate
14. syrup
15. machine

Write on Your Own
page 43
Sets of directions will vary. Students should use four Core Words.

Writing directions usually means putting steps in chronological order. Students needing help with this organization might be asked to begin sentences with the words *First, Second,* and *Third.* Check that student directions are in a logical order.

Proofreading Practice
1–4. recipe, busy, dozen, separate

REVIEW LESSON 12

1. reindeer
2. sleeves
3. retreat
4. great
5. quote
6. stride
7. motor
8. hotel
9. truth
10. smooth
11. unite
12. usual
13. purpose
14. turkey
15. burden
16. current
17. tongue
18. beige
19. syrup
20. recipe

LESSON 13

Focus
page 46

1–15. cr)uel, thr)oat, gr)eedy, sw)allow, br)oken, st)ubborn, cl)inic, st)umble, cl)othing, st)eeple, cl)over, st)artle, bl)ister, sp)arkle, fl)avor
16–20. dr)izzle, cr)ystal, cl)assify, bl)ueprint, str)ength

Words and Meanings
page 47
1. clothing
2. clinic
3. broken
4. stumble
5. blister
6. steeple
7. startle
8. stubborn
9. sparkle
10. throat
11. cruel
12. swallow
13. clover
14. greedy
15. flavor

Word Works
16. peaceful
17. powerful
18. joyful
19. stressful
20. colorful
21. hopeful
22. painful
23. successful
24. delightful

Word Play
page 48
1. startle
2. blister
3. greedy
4. throat
5. stubborn
6. broken
7. clothing
8. clover
9. steeple
10. clinic
11. flavor
12. swallow
13. stumble
14. cruel
15. sparkle

Write on Your Own
page 49
Lists of rules will vary. Students should use four Core Words.

Check each list item to see if it contains a complete thought.

Proofreading Practice
1–4. throat, clinic, broken, cruel
5. eats.
6. animal
7. Don't

LESSON 14

Focus
page 50

1–9. hour, pouch, crouch, blouse, amount, outward, thousand, pronounce, account
10–15. however, coward, powder, shower, towel, browse
16–20. b)ough), bloodh)oun)d, ast)ou)nding, ch)ow)der, all)ow)ance

Words and Meanings
page 51
1. shower
2. towel
3. hour
4. browse
5. however
6. pouch
7. blouse
8. coward
9. powder
10. pronounce
11. outward
12. crouch
13. thousand
14. amount
15. account

Word Works
16. upward
17. inward
18. afterward
19. eastward
20. westward
21. northward
22. southward
23. skyward
24. earthward
25. sideward

Word Play
page 52
1. powder
2. coward
3. towel
4. amount
5. browse
6. account
7. however
8. towel
9. pronounce
10. crouch
11. outward
12. save now
13. hour
14. coward
15. shower
16. towel
17. thousand
18. pouch
19. blouse
20. however

Write on Your Own
page 53
Descriptions will vary. Students should use four Core Words.

Challenge students to make their descriptions appeal to all five senses. Check descriptions for sensory modifiers.

Proofreading Practice
1–5. amount, blouse, towel, hour, browse

LESSON 15

Focus
page 54

1–5. title, stable, middle, waffle, cable
6–11. mammal, sandal, local, trial, metal, signal
12–15. barrel, marvel, level, model
16–20. grumb)le), sever)al), lab)el), miss)ile) tremb)le)

Words and Meanings
page 55
1. marvel
2. signal
3. local
4. cable
5. title
6. mammal
7. metal
8. waffle
9. middle
10. level
11. stable
12. model
13. sandal
14. barrel
15. trial

Word Works
16. personal
17. clinical
18. coastal
19. natural
20. musical
21. magical
22. national
23. global
24. familial

Word Play
page 56
1. waffle
2. stable
3. mammal
4. marvel
5. trial
6. middle
7. cable
8. sandal
9. barrel
10. local
11. title, trial
12. waffle, model
13. level, metal
14. middle, signal
15. stable, cable
16. noun, verb
17. noun, verb, adjective
18. noun
19. adjective, noun
20. noun, adjective, verb

Write on Your Own
page 57
Scripts will vary. Students should use four Core Words. For peer assessment, have students read their scripts aloud.

Proofreading Practice
1–4. metal, level, cable, signal
5. ASTRONAUT: This
6. Perez
7. though.
8. crew.

LESSON 16

Focus
page 58

1–15. p)our), p)ar)cel, w)ar)m, t)ar)get, f)or)ce, n)or)mal,)or)bit, c)ar)pet, ad)or)e,)ar)tist, aff)or)d, st)ar)ve, m)or)tal, d)oor)bell, m)ar)ket
16–20. b)ar)becue, p)or)cupine, c)our)ty)ar)d,)ar)gument, c)or)ral

Words and Meanings
page 59
1. warm
2. normal
3. adore
4. force
5. doorbell
6. orbit
7. carpet
8. mortal
9. target
10. artist
11. afford
12. starve
13. market
14. pour
15. parcel

Word Works
16. endanger
17. enable
18. enslave
19. enlarge
20. entrap
21. enrich
22. ensure
23. encircle
24. entangle

Word Play
page 60
1–7. parcel, normal, artist, afford, mortal, doorbell, market
8. starve
9. pour
10. warm
11. force
12–15. target, orbit, carpet, adore

Write on Your Own
page 61
Memoirs will vary. Students should use four Core Words. Check memoirs for students' abilities to use descriptive words in a personal experience. For peer evaluation, have students read their memoirs to one another.

Proofreading Practice
1–5. adore, mortal, orbit, normal, afford

LESSON 17

Focus
page 62

1–15. real, reel; tide, tied; horse, hoarse; plane, plain; break, brake; throne, thrown; (petal), (pedal), (peddle)

16–20. wade, weighed, weather, whether, (mussels)

Words and Meanings
page 63

1. throne
2. horse
3. tide
4. petal
5. thrown
6. tied
7. plane
8. hoarse
9. reel
10. brake
11. break
12. plain
13. pedal
14. real
15. peddle

Word Works

16. popularity
17. solidity
18. finality
19. mortality
20. similarity
21. generality
22. normality
23. brutality
24. originality

Word Play
page 64

1. peddle
2. real
3. tied
4. plain
5. thrown
6. break
7. plane
8. petal
9. tide
10. pedal
11. throne
12. reel
13. horse, hoarse
14. real, reel
15. pedal, peddle
16. break, brake

Write on Your Own
page 65

Poems will vary. Students should use four Core Words. For peer evaluation, students can share their poems with one another.

Proofreading Practice

1–5. break, hoarse, plain, thrown, reel

REVIEW LESSON 18

1. throat
2. flavor
3. clover
4. broken
5. pronounce
6. hour
7. shower
8. browse
9. mammal
10. stable
11. middle
12. sandal
13. normal
14. adore
15. mortal
16. artist
17. real
18. break
19. plain
20. tied

LESSON 19

Focus
page 68

1–15. waited, (tracing), wagged, followed, (handling), planned, paying, stepping, hanging, shopping, crawling, dropped gardening, weeding, whispering

16–20. (battling), (choosing), remembered, (meddling), referring

Words and Meanings
page 69

1. waited
2. gardening
3. planned
4. shopping
5. paying
6. weeding
7. crawling
8. handling
9. tracing
10. dropped
11. stepping
12. hanging
13. wagged
14. whispering
15. followed

Word Works

16. one who waits
17. one who follows
18. one who pays
19. one who handles
20. one who gardens
21. one who plans
22. one who peddles
23. one who loses
24. one who bikes

Word Play
page 70

1. followed
2. crawling
3. planned
4. gardening
5. waited
6. paying
7. whispering
8. dropped
9. handling
10. wagged
11. weeding
12. stepping
13. shopping
14. paying
15. hanging
16. gardening
17. crawling
18. followed
19. tracing
20. shopping

Write on Your Own
page 71

Stories will vary. Students should use four Core Words.

For assessment have students read their stories to someone else. Have volunteers read their classmates' stories aloud.

Proofreading Practice

1–5. hanging, dropped, Crawling, planned, waited

LESSON 20

Focus
page 72

1–7. potato, zero, tomato, piano, hero, radio, echo

8–15. (potatoes), zeros, (tomatoes), pianos, (heroes), radios, (echoes), (mosquitoes)

16–20. studio(s), centuries, rodeo(s), glossaries, dynamo(s)

Words and Meanings
page 73

1. heroes
2. radio
3. hero
4. echo
5. echoes
6. radios
7. piano
8. pianos
9. zero
10. zeros
11. mosquitoes
12. tomato
13. potato
14. tomatoes
15. potatoes

Word Works

16. historic
17. cubic
18. magnetic
19. artistic
20. angelic
21. melodic
22. oceanic
23. climatic
24. tragic

Word Play
page 74

1. radios
2. piano
3. radio
4. echoes
5. zero
6. potatoes
7. mosquitoes
8. pianos
9. tomatoes
10. a nice tune
11. echo
12. zeros
13. potato
14. heroes
15. tomato
16–18. Answers will vary.

Write on Your Own
page 75

Announcements will vary. Students should use four Core Words.

Have students use a who, what, and where checklist as they revise to be sure they have included all important information.

Proofreading Practice

1–4. echo, heroes, pianos, radio
5. Sunday
6. June 5, 1994
7. Scalzi Park
8. Portland, Maine

LESSON 21

Focus
page 76

1–6. among, award, arise, amuse, agree, asleep

7–15. beginning, believe, betray, between, behave, behind, belong, beyond, become

16–20. beneath, bewilder, (above), bewitch, bestow

Words and Meanings
page 77

1. amuse
2. asleep
3. beyond
4. become
5. believe
6. agree
7. among
8. between
9. arise
10. behave
11. behind
12. betray
13. belong
14. award
15. beginning

Word Works

16. the state of being agreed
17. the state of being disappointed
18. the state of being excited
19. the state of being contented
20. the state of being amazed
21. the state of being puzzled
22. the state of being employed

Word Play
page 78

1. beyond
2. among
3. betray
4. agree
5. become
6. belong
7. award
8–9. arise, behind
10. beginning
11. amuse
12. believe
13. between
14. behave
15. asleep

Write on Your Own
page 79

Journal entries will vary. Students should use four Core Words.

Check entries for students' abilities to maintain a consistent point of view.

Proofreading Practice

1–5. beginning, beyond, behind, between, asleep

LESSON 22

Focus
page 80

1–10. referee's, officer's, director's, actress's, waiter's, owner's, pilot's, actor's, lady's, baby's

11–15. babies', ladies', parents', buyers', students'

16–20. athletes', (octopus's), astronauts', (triceratops's), operators'

Words and Meanings
page 81

1. director's
2. students'
3. parents'
4. actress's
5. actor's
6. officer's
7. referee's
8. waiter's
9. pilot's
10. baby's
11. babies'
12. ladies'
13. lady's
14. owner's
15. buyers'

Work Works

16. geese's
17. women's
18. mice's
19. teeth's
20. men's

Word Play
page 82

1. Parents'
2. Baby's
3. Officer's
4. Owner's
5. Pilot's
6. Students'
7. waiter's
8. buyers'
9–10. babies', ladies'
11–12. lady's, baby's
13–14. actress's, actor's
15. referee's
16. director's

Write on Your Own
page 83

The articles will vary. Students should write four Core Words.

Review articles for who, what, where, when, and why information about the event.

Proofreading Practice

1–5. buyers', referee's, parents', waiter's, students'

LESSON 23

Focus
page 84

1–4. lungs, skull, nerves, vein

5–10. tendons, plasma, marrow, kidney, stomach, tonsils

11–15. ligament, appendix, spinal cord, skeleton, artery

16–20. muscles, esophagus, verte(br)ae, (bl)ood/(str)eam, epidermis

Words and Meanings
page 85

1. skull
2. nerves
3. tonsils
4. artery
5. vein
6. plasma
7. lungs
8. stomach
9. kidney
10. appendix
11. skeleton
12. marrow
13. spinal cord
14. ligament
15. tendons

Word Works

16. tonsil/tonsils
17. tendon/tendons
18. appendix

Word Play
page 86

1. tonsils
2. lungs
3. stomach
4. appendix
5–9. skull, plasma, spinal cord, skeleton, stomach
10–12. skull, appendix, marrow
13. vein
14. nerves
15. ligament
16. tendons
17. artery
18. kidney
19. skel/e/ton
20. lig/a/ment
21. stom/ach
22. ap/pen/dix

Write on Your Own
page 87

Lists will vary. Students should use four Core Words.

This writing assignment can focus on using the imperative sentence. Have students work on setting the tone of the brochure by beginning each item in the list with a strong verb. Check lists for verb usage.

Proofreading Practice

1–4. nerves, artery, spinal cord, skull
5. straight.
6. bike?

REVIEW LESSON 24

1. planned
2. gardening
3. dropped
4. tracing
5. tomatoes
6. zeros
7. heroes
8. pianos
9. amuse
10. behave
11. believe
12. asleep
13. babies'
14. buyers'
15. actor's
16. director's
17. lungs
18. nerves
19. marrow
20. stomach

LESSON 25

Focus
page 90

1–8. disconnect, disappear, disagree, discover, disloyal, displease, disgrace, distrust

9–15. misjudge, mislaid, mislead, misprint, mismatch, misspell, mistreat

16–20. (mis)fortune, (dis)appoint, (mis)pronounce, (dis)honest, (mis)understand

Words and Meanings
page 91

1. displease
2. misprint
3. misspell
4. disconnect
5. mislaid
6. disappear
7. disgrace
8. disloyal
9. mistreat
10. mislead
11. discover
12. distrust
13. mismatch
14. disagree
15. misjudge

Word Works

16. misbehave
17. misstate
18. misread
19. misuse
20. disapprove
21. discomfort
22. disbelieve

Word Play
page 92

1–8. misprint, distrust, disagree, mislaid, mistreat, discover, mislead, disloyal

9. misjudge
10–12. disconnect, disappear, misspell
13. disgrace
14. displease
15. mismatch
16. file in a wrong way
17. view ahead of time
18. place again
19. not even
20. the opposite of sense

Write on Your Own
page 93

Reviews will vary. Students should use four Core Words.

Check reviews for students' abilities to use critical judgment as opposed to simply a summary of the show.

Proofreading Practice

1–5. disagree, mislaid, disappear, disconnect, discover

LESSON 26

Focus
page 94

1–12. falc(o)n, stadi(u)m, ball(a)d, s(u)ppose, hast(e)n, apr(o)n, peri(o)d, ball(o)t, cany(o)n, org(a)n, parr(o)t, cart(o)n

13–15. capt(ai)n, mount(ai)n, vill(ai)n

16–20. oxyg(e)n, pig(eo)n, p(o)llute, med(i)cine, pelic(a)n

Words and Meanings
page 95

1. apron
2. hasten
3. stadium
4. captain
5. mountain
6. villain
7. ballad
8. carton
9. ballot
10. organ
11. period
12. suppose
13. parrot
14. falcon
15. canyon

Word Works

16. organist
17. typist
18. cyclist
19. pianist
20. tourist

Word Play
page 96

1. parrot
2. ballot
3. ballad
4. carton
5. apron
6. captain
7. organ
8. period
9. canyon
10. suppose
11. villain
12. falcon/parrot
13. hasten
14. mountain
15–16. stadium, period

Write on Your Own
page 97

Announcements will vary. Students should use four Core Words.

Check announcements to see if students have included information about who, what, when, where, and why.

Proofreading Practice

1–4. Canyon, period, captain, carton
5. paid.
6. Grover Stadium
7. The rest
8. Food.

LESSON 27

Focus
page 98

1–12. recent, absent, confident, represent, different, apparent, accident, evident, resident, prominent, dependent, permanent

13–15. important, tolerant, assistant

16–20. effic(ie)nt, immigr(a)nt, indign(a)nt, transpar(e)nt, signific(a)nt

Words and Meanings
page 99

1. recent
2. absent
3. assistant
4. represent
5. prominent
6. apparent/evident
7. permanent
8. resident
9. confident
10. dependent
11. accident
12. important
13. tolerant
14. different
15. evident/apparent

Word Works

16. confidence
17. difference
18. importance
19. tolerance
20. evidence
21. prominence
22. dependence
23. permanence
24. absence

Word Play
page 100

1. confident
2. tolerant
3. important
4. different
5. resident
6. absent
7. accident
8. assistant
9. permanent
10. dependent
11. recent
12. prominent
13. apparent
14. evident
15. represent
16. perm(a)(e)nt
17. (a)ppar(e)nt
18. accid(e)nt
19. depend(e)nt
20. prom(i)(e)nt

Write on Your Own
page 101

Speeches will vary. Students should use four Core Words. Check speeches for strong beginnings.

Proofreading Practice

1–5. confident, evident, recent, assistant, absent

LESSON 28

Focus
page 102

1–15. rain/coat, hand/shake, motor/cycle, road/block, bed/spread, birth/place, arrow/head, half/back, earth/quake, news/paper, flood/light, under/brush, sweat/shirt, draw/bridge, sun/glasses

16–20. trouble/maker, snap/shot, body/guard, needle/point, straight/forward

Words and Meanings
page 103

1. handshake
2. birthplace
3. drawbridge
4. motorcycle
5. roadblock
6. floodlight
7. bedspread
8. raincoat
9. halfback
10. sweatshirt
11. sunglasses
12. arrowhead
13. underbrush
14. earthquake
15. newspaper

Word Works

16. cardboard
17. backyard
18. toothbrush
19. foghorn
20. snowstorm

Word Play
page 104

1. sunglasses
2. arrowhead
3. newspaper
4. raincoat
5. floodlight
6. halfback
7. drawbridge
8. sweatshirt
9–10. birthplace, earthquake
11. motorcycle
12. bedspread
13. underbrush
14. handshake
15. roadblock

Write on Your Own
page 105

Letters will vary. Students should use four Core Words.

Check to see if students have included the writer's address, a date, a salutation, and a complimentary close.

Proofreading Practice

1–4. earthquake, newspaper, drawbridge, sunglasses
5. newspaper?
6. Mrs. Chang's

LESSON 29

Focus
page 106

1–5. laser, sonar, combine, airplane, radar

6–12. gravity, camera, telephone, transistor, microchip, skyscraper, microscope

13–14. automobile, television

15. electricity

16–20. antibiotics, submarine, helicopter, refrigeration, stethoscope

Words and Meanings
page 107

1. skyscraper
2. combine
3. camera
4. telephone
5. electricity
6. transistor
7. television
8. radar
9. sonar
10. automobile
11. airplane
12. gravity
13. microscope
14. laser
15. microchip

Word Works
16. microfilm
17. microwave
18. microsecond

Word Play
page 108

1. automobile
2. combine
3. electricity
4. laser
5. microchip
6. microscope
7. radar
8. skyscraper
9. sonar
10. telephone
11. television
12. gravity
13. airplane
14. transistor
15. camera
16. a farm machine that harvests and threshes grain
17. to join together; unite
18. the force that pulls things toward the center of Earth
19. serious nature
20. to talk with someone by telephone

Write on Your Own
page 109

Essays will vary. Students should use four Core Words.

Check essays to see if students have stuck to the topic.

Proofreading Practice

1–5. airplane, telephone, camera, microchip, electricity

REVIEW LESSON 30

1. disgrace
2. disagree
3. mislaid
4. mistrust
5. hasten
6. mountain
7. ballad
8. falcon
9. different
10. absent
11. confident
12. recent
13. raincoat
14. bedspread
15. drawbridge
16. newspaper
17. television
18. electricity
19. laser
20. camera

LESSON 31

Focus
page 112

1–15. fo(l)k, de(b)t, colum(n), (w)rench, (g)naw, ai(s)(l)e, (w)rinkle, autum(n), dou(b)t, r(h)yme, bris(t)le, s(w)ord, (g)narled, lis(t)en, (w)res(t)le

16–17. solemn, condemn

18–20. campaign, rhythm, foreign

Words and Meanings
page 113

1. folk
2. bristle
3. autumn
4. column
5. sword
6. aisle
7. doubt
8. wrinkle
9. gnarled
10. listen
11. gnaw
12. wrench
13. wrestle
14. rhyme
15. debt

Word Works
16. unwrinkled
17. indebted
18. encouraging
19. mismanagement
20. recycler
21. impossibility
22. distasteful
23. insincerely
24. unheroic

Word Play
page 114

1–7. folk, debt, aisle, doubt, rhyme, sword, wrestle
8. bristle
9. gnarled
10. column
11–13. gnaw, autumn, sword
14. listen
15. wrench
16. wrinkle

Write on Your Own
page 115

Stories will vary. Students should use four Core Words. Use this activity to assess students' abilities to write and punctuate dialogue.

Proofreading Practice

1–5. autumn, listen, gnaw, sword, debt

LESSON 32

Focus
page 116

1–11. orphan, geography, elephant, alphabet, paragraph, telegraph, nephew, phantom, photograph, dolphin, triumph

12–15. laugh, tough, enough, trough

16–20. as(ph)alt, ty(ph)oon, (ph)armacy, rou(gh), trium(ph)ant

Words and Meanings
page 117

1. nephew
2. orphan
3. elephant
4. paragraph
5. tough
6. alphabet
7. geography
8. dolphin
9. telegraph
10. phantom
11. triumph
12. trough
13. laugh
14. photograph
15. enough

Word Works
16. telephoto
17. telecast
18. telemeter
19. telemarketer
20. teleprinter

Word Play
page 118

1. telegraph
2. enough
3. geography
4. photograph
5. triumph
6. elephant
7. nephew
8. alphabet
9. dolphin
10. laugh
11–12. paragraph, phantom
13–15. tough, triumph, trough
16. orphan

Write on Your Own
page 119

Interviews will vary. Students should use four Core Words. For peer evaluation, have students read their interviews aloud with a partner.

Proofreading Practice

1–5. laugh, enough, elephant, alphabet, trough
6. tough?
7. Just
8. act.

LESSON 33

Focus
page 120

1–9. edition, discussion, position, promotion, mission, selection, tradition, examination, restriction

10–15. explosion, measure, collision, version, pleasure, treasure

16–20. commotion, construction, estimation, limitation, observation

Words and Meanings
page 121

1. measure
2. pleasure
3. discussion
4. version
5. tradition
6. selection
7. examination
8. edition
9. promotion
10. position
11. treasure
12. mission
13. collision
14. explosion
15. restriction

Word Works

16. honorary
17. legendary
18. momentary
19. customary
20. visionary

Word Play
page 122

1. edition
2. treasure
3. explosion
4. collision
5. version
6. measure
7. discussion
8. mission
9. restriction
10. pleasure
11. mission
12. position
13. promotion
14. examination
15. selection
16. tradition
17. discussion
18. collision

Write on Your Own
page 123

Book-jacket blurbs will vary. Students should use four Core Words.

For self-evaluation, encourage students to add a picture to their book jacket and display finished work on a bulletin board. If possible, secure copies of the books and compare any jacket copy or similar descriptions provided by the publisher.

Proofreading Practice

1–4. mission, edition, treasure, selection

LESSON 34

Focus
page 124

1–11. yards, quart, acre, teaspoon, ounces, gallon, liter, bushels, meter, minutes, volume

12–15. millimeter, centimeter, (tablespoon), kilometer

16–20. leagues, eon, degree, decades, amperes

Words and Meanings
page 125

1. acre
2. tablespoon
3. teaspoon
4. yards
5. volume
6. meter
7. centimeter
8. millimeter
9. minutes
10. liter
11. kilometer
12. bushels
13. ounces
14. quart
15. gallon

Word Works

16. kilometer
17. centimeter
18. millimeter
19. centiliter
20. kilogram
21. milliliter
22. centigram
23. kiloliter

Word Play
page 126

1. ounces
2. quart
3. tablespoon
4. gallon
5. yards
6. acre
7. teaspoon
8. volume
9. millimeter
10. centimeter
11. kilometer
12. bushels
13. liter
14. minutes
15. meter
16. a written report of what was said and done at a meeting
17. the basic pattern of rhythm that accented notes or beats give to a piece of music
18. the amount of sound

Write on Your Own
page 127

Inventories will vary. Students should use four Core Words. For a peer assessment, have students compare their inventories and note the most unusual items listed.

Proofreading Practice

1–5. quart, minutes, gallon, centimeter, acre

LESSON 35

Focus
page 128

1–10. Grand Canyon, Bryce Canyon, Grand Teton, Glacier Bay, Crater Lake, Petrified Forest, Hawaii Volcanoes, Carlsbad Caverns, Mammoth Cave, Mount Rainier

11–15. Yosemite, Everglades, Badlands, Acadia, Sequoia

16–17. adventure, equipment

18–20. parka, compass, canteen

Words and Meanings
page 129

1. Everglades
2. Acadia
3. Badlands
4. Mammoth Cave
5. Carlsbad Caverns
6. Grand Canyon
7. Petrified Forest
8. Bryce Canyon
9. Grand Teton
10. Sequoia
11. Yosemite
12. Crater Lake
13. Mount Rainier
14. Glacier Bay
15. Hawaii Volcanoes

Word Works

16. firewood
17. campsite
18. sunrise
19. postcard
20. backpack
21. moonlight
22. matchstick
23. waterfall
24. hummingbird

Word Play
page 130

1. Hawaii Volcanoes
2. Petrified Forest
3. Crater Lake
4. Everglades
5. Grand Teton
6. Glacier Bay
7. Mount Rainier
8. Bryce Canyon
9. Carlsbad Caverns
10. Yosemite
11. wilderness
12. Badlands
13. Acadia
14. Sequoia
15. Grand Canyon
16. Mammoth Cave

Write on Your Own
page 131

Itineraries will vary. Students should use four Core Words. Check drafts for logical order of events.

Proofreading Practice

1–4. Mount Rainier, Crater Lake, Sequoia, Yosemite
5. Seattle, Washington
6. Oregon
7. California
8. July

REVIEW LESSON 36

1. folk
2. debt
3. rhyme
4. sword
5. laugh
6. enough
7. phantom
8. triumph
9. measure
10. collision
11. examination
12. discussion
13. gallon
14. yards
15. acre
16. bushels
17. Carlsbad Caverns
18. Grand Teton
19. Hawaii Volcanoes
20. Yosemite

McGRAW-HILL LEARNING MATERIALS
Offers a selection of workbooks to meet all your needs.

Look for all of these fine educational workbooks
in the McGraw-Hill Learning Materials SPECTRUM Series.
All workbooks meet school curriculum guidelines and correspond to
The McGraw-Hill Companies classroom textbooks.

SPECTRUM GEOGRAPHY – NEW FOR 1998!

Full-color, three-part lessons strengthen geography knowledge and map reading skills. Focusing on five geographic themes including location, place, human/environmental interaction, movement and regions. Over 150 pages. Glossary of geographical terms and answer key included.

TITLE	ISBN	PRICE
Grade 3, Communities	1-57768-153-3	$7.95
Grade 4, Regions	1-57768-154-1	$7.95
Grade 5, USA	1-57768-155-X	$7.95
Grade 6, World	1-57768-156-8	$7.95

SPECTRUM MATH

Features easy-to-follow instructions that give students a clear path to success. This series has comprehensive coverage of the basic skills, helping children to master math fundamentals. Over 150 pages. Answer key included.

TITLE	ISBN	PRICE
Grade 1	1-57768-111-8	$6.95
Grade 2	1-57768-112-6	$6.95
Grade 3	1-57768-113-4	$6.95
Grade 4	1-57768-114-2	$6.95
Grade 5	1-57768-115-0	$6.95
Grade 6	1-57768-116-9	$6.95
Grade 7	1-57768-117-7	$6.95
Grade 8	1-57768-118-5	$6.95

SPECTRUM PHONICS

Provides everything children need to build multiple skills in language. Focusing on phonics, structural analysis, and dictionary skills, this series also offers creative ideas for using phonics and word study skills in other language arts. Over 200 pages. Answer key included.

TITLE	ISBN	PRICE
Grade K	1-57768-120-7	$6.95
Grade 1	1-57768-121-5	$6.95
Grade 2	1-57768-122-3	$6.95
Grade 3	1-57768-123-1	$6.95
Grade 4	1-57768-124-X	$6.95
Grade 5	1-57768-125-8	$6.95
Grade 6	1-57768-126-6	$6.95

SPECTRUM READING

This full-color series creates an enjoyable reading environment, even for below-average readers. Each book contains captivating content, colorful characters, and compelling illustrations, so children are eager to find out what happens next. Over 150 pages. Answer key included.

TITLE	ISBN	PRICE
Grade K	1-57768-130-4	$6.95
Grade 1	1-57768-131-2	$6.95
Grade 2	1-57768-132-0	$6.95
Grade 3	1-57768-133-9	$6.95
Grade 4	1-57768-134-7	$6.95
Grade 5	1-57768-135-5	$6.95
Grade 6	1-57768-136-3	$6.95

SPECTRUM SPELLING – NEW FOR 1998!

This series links spelling to reading and writing and increases skills in words and meanings, consonant and vowel spellings and proofreading practice. Over 200 pages in full color. Speller dictionary and answer key included.

TITLE	ISBN	PRICE
Grade 1	1-57768-161-4	$7.95
Grade 2	1-57768-162-2	$7.95
Grade 3	1-57768-163-0	$7.95
Grade 4	1-57768-164-9	$7.95
Grade 5	1-57768-165-7	$7.95
Grade 6	1-57768-166-5	$7.95

SPECTRUM WRITING

Lessons focus on creative and expository writing using clearly stated objectives and pre-writing exercises. Eight essential reading skills are applied. Activities include main idea, sequence, comparison, detail, fact and opinion, cause and effect, and making a point. Over 130 pages. Answer key included.

TITLE	ISBN	PRICE
Grade 1	1-57768-141-X	$6.95
Grade 2	1-57768-142-8	$6.95
Grade 3	1-57768-143-6	$6.95
Grade 4	1-57768-144-4	$6.95
Grade 5	1-57768-145-2	$6.95
Grade 6	1-57768-146-0	$6.95
Grade 7	1-57768-147-9	$6.95
Grade 8	1-57768-148-7	$6.95

SPECTRUM TEST PREP from the Nation's #1 Testing Company

Prepares children to do their best on current editions of the five major standardized tests. Activities reinforce test-taking skills through examples, tips, practice and timed exercises. Subjects include reading, math and language. 150 pages. Answer key included.

TITLE	ISBN	PRICE
Grade 3	1-57768-103-7	$8.95
Grade 4	1-57768-104-5	$8.95
Grade 5	1-57768-105-3	$8.95
Grade 6	1-57768-106-1	$8.95
Grade 7	1-57768-107-X	$8.95
Grade 8	1-57768-108-8	$8.95

Look for these other fine educational series available from McGRAW-HILL LEARNING MATERIALS.

BASIC SKILLS CURRICULUM

A complete basic skills curriculum, a school year's worth of practice! This series reinforces necessary skills in the following categories: reading comprehension, vocabulary, grammar, writing, math applications, problem solving, test taking and more. Over 700 pages. Answer key included.

TITLE	ISBN	PRICE
Grade 3 – new for 1998!	1-57768-093-6	$19.95
Grade 4 – new for 1998!	1-57768-094-4	$19.95
Grade 5 – new for 1998!	1-57768-095-2	$19.95
Grade 6 – new for 1998!	1-57768-096-0	$19.95
Grade 7	1-57768-097-9	$19.95
Grade 8	1-57768-098-7	$19.95

BUILDING SKILLS MATH

Six basic skills practice books give children the reinforcement they need to master math concepts. Each single-skill lesson consists of a worked example as well as self-directing and self-correcting exercises. 48pages. Answer key included.

TITLE	ISBN	PRICE
Grade 3	1-57768-053-7	$2.49
Grade 4	1-57768-054-5	$2.49
Grade 5	1-57768-055-3	$2.49
Grade 6	1-57768-056-1	$2.49
Grade 7	1-57768-057-X	$2.49
Grade 8	1-57768-058-8	$2.49

BUILDING SKILLS READING

Children master eight crucial reading comprehension skills by working with true stories and exciting adventure tales. 48pages. Answer key included.

TITLE	ISBN	PRICE
Grade 3	1-57768-063-4	$2.49
Grade 4	1-57768-064-2	$2.49
Grade 5	1-57768-065-0	$2.49
Grade 6	1-57768-066-9	$2.49
Grade 7	1-57768-067-7	$2.49
Grade 8	1-57768-068-5	$2.49

BUILDING SKILLS PROBLEM SOLVING

These self-directed practice books help students master the most important step in math – how to think a problem through. Each workbook contains 20 lessons that teach specific problem solving skills including understanding the question, identifying extra information, and multi-step problems. 48pages. Answer key included.

TITLE	ISBN	PRICE
Grade 3	1-57768-073-1	$2.49
Grade 4	1-57768-074-X	$2.49
Grade 5	1-57768-075-8	$2.49
Grade 6	1-57768-076-6	$2.49
Grade 7	1-57768-077-4	$2.49
Grade 8	1-57768-078-2	$2.49

THE McGRAW-HILL
JUNIOR ACADEMIC™ WORKBOOK SERIES

An exciting new partnership between the world's #1 educational publisher and the world's premiere entertainment company brings the respective strengths and reputation of each great media company to the educational publishing arena. McGraw-Hill and Warner Bros. have partnered to provide high-quality educational materials in a fun and entertaining way.

For more than 110 years, school children have been exposed to McGraw-Hill educational products. This new educational workbook series addresses the educational needs of young children, ages three through eight, stimulating their love of learning in an entertaining way that features Warner Bros.' beloved Looney Tunes™ and Animaniacs™ cartoon characters.

The McGraw-Hill Junior Academic™ Workbook Series features twenty books – four books for five age groups including toddler, preschool, kindergarten, first grade and second grade. Each book has up to 80 pages of full-color lessons such as: colors, numbers, shapes and the alphabet for toddlers; and math, reading, phonics, thinking skills, and vocabulary for preschoolers through grade two.

This fun and educational workbook series will be available in bookstores, mass market retail outlets, teacher supply stores and children's specialty stores in summer 1998. Look for them at a store near you, and look for some serious fun!

TODDLER SERIES
32-page workbooks featuring the Baby Looney Tunes™

	ISBN	PRICE
My Colors Go 'Round	1-57768-208-4	$2.25
My 1, 2, 3's	1-57768-218-1	$2.25
My A, B, C's	1-57768-228-9	$2.25
My Ups & Downs	1-57768-238-6	$2.25

PRESCHOOL SERIES
80-page workbooks featuring the Looney Tunes™

	ISBN	PRICE
Math	1-57768-209-2	$2.99
Reading	1-57768-219-X	$2.99
Vowel Sounds	1-57768-229-7	$2.99
Sound Patterns	1-57768-239-4	$2.99

KINDERGARTEN SERIES
80-page workbooks featuring the Looney Tunes™

	ISBN	PRICE
Math	1-57768-200-9	$2.99
Reading	1-57768-210-6	$2.99
Phonics	1-57768-220-3	$2.99
Thinking Skills	1-57768-230-0	$2.99

GRADE 1 SERIES

80-page workbooks featuring the Animaniacs™

	ISBN	PRICE
Math	1-57768-201-7	$2.99
Reading	1-57768-211-4	$2.99
Phonics	1-57768-221-1	$2.99
Word Builders	1-57768-231-9	$2.99

GRADE 2 SERIES

80-page workbooks featuring the Animaniacs™

	ISBN	PRICE
Math	1-57768-202-5	$2.99
Reading	1-57768-212-2	$2.99
Phonics	1-57768-222-X	$2.99
Word Builders	1-57768-232-7	$2.99

SOFTWARE TITLES AVAILABLE FROM McGRAW-HILL HOME INTERACTIVE

The skills taught in school are now available at home! These titles are now available in retail stores and teacher supply stores everywhere.
All titles meet school guidelines and are based on
The McGraw-Hill Companies classroom software titles.

MATH GRADES 1 & 2

These math programs are a great way to teach and reinforce skills used in everyday situations. Fun, friendly characters need help with their math skills. Everyone's friend, Nubby the stubby pencil, will help kids master the math in the Numbers Quiz show. Foggy McHammer, a carpenter, needs some help building his playhouse so that all the boards will fit together! Julio Bambino's kitchen antics will surely burn his pastries if you don't help him set the clock timer correctly! We can't forget Turbo Tomato, a fruit with a passion for adventure who needs help calculating his daredevil stunts.

Math Grades 1 & 2 use a tested, proven approach to reinforcing your child's math skills while keeping them intrigued with Nubby and his collection of crazy friends.

TITLE	ISBN	PRICE
Grade 1: Nubby's Quiz Show	1-57768-011-1	$19.95
Grade 2: Foggy McHammer's Treehouse	1-57768-012-X	$19.95

MISSION MASTERS™ MATH AND LANGUAGE ARTS

The Mission Masters™ -- Pauline, Rakeem, Mia, and T.J. – need your help. The Mission Masters™ are a team of young agents working for the Intelliforce Agency, a high level cooperative whose goal is to maintain order on our rather unruly planet. From within the agency's top secret Command Control Center, the agency's central computer, M5, has detected a threat… and guess what – you're the agent assigned to the mission!

MISSION MASTERS™ MATH GRADES 3, 4 & 5

This series of exciting activities encourages young mathematicians to challenge themselves and their math skills to overcome the perils of villains and other planetary threats. Skills reinforced include: analyzing and solving real world problems, estimation, measurements, geometry, whole numbers, fractions, graphs, and patterns.

TITLE	ISBN	PRICE
Grade 3: Mission Masters™ Defeat Dirty D!	1-57768-013-8	$29.95
Grade 4: Mission Masters™ Alien Encounter	1-57768-014-6	$29.95
Grade 5: Mission Masters™ Meet Mudflat Moe	1-57768-015-4	$29.95

MISSION MASTERS™ LANGUAGE ARTS GRADES 3, 4 & 5 – COMING IN 1998!

This new series invites children to apply their language skills to defeat unscrupulous characters and to overcome other earthly dangers. Skills reinforced include language mechanics and usage, punctuation, spelling, vocabulary, reading comprehension and creative writing.

TITLE	ISBN	PRICE
Grade 3: Mission Masters™ Feeding Frenzy	1-57768-023-5	$29.95
Grade 4: Mission Masters™ Network Nightmare	1-57768-024-3	$29.95
Grade 5: Mission Masters™ Mummy Mysteries	1-57768-025-1	$29.95

FAHRENHEITS' FABULOUS FORTUNE

Aunt and Uncle Fahrenheit have passed on and left behind an enormous fortune. They always believed that only the wise should be wealthy, and luckily for you, you're the smartest kid in the family. Now, you must prove your intelligence in order to be the rightful heir. Using the principles of physical science, master each of the challenges that they left behind in the abandoned mansion and you will earn digits to the security code that seals your treasure.

This fabulous physical science program introduces kids to the basics as they build skills in everything from data collection and analysis to focused subjects such as electricity and energy. Multi-step problem-solving activities encourage creativity and critical thinking while children enthusiastically accept the challenges in order to solve the mysteries of the mansion. Based on the #1 Physical Science Textbook from McGraw-Hill!

TITLE	ISBN	PRICE
Fahrenheit's Fabulous Fortune	1-57768-009-X	$29.95
Physical Science, Grades 8 & Up		

All titles for Windows 3.1™, Windows '95™, and Macintosh™.

Visit us on the Internet at

www.mhhi.com